HOW TO DOUBLE
YOUR CHILD'S
GRADES
IN SCHOOL

*the text of this book is printed
on 100% recycled paper*

HOW TO DOUBLE YOUR CHILD'S GRADES IN SCHOOL

BY

EUGENE M. SCHWARTZ

BARNES & NOBLE BOOKS

A DIVISION OF HARPER & ROW, PUBLISHERS

New York, Evanston, San Francisco, London

TO MY SON MICHAEL.

May he learn ten times as much
as his father, because in his
world he'll need every fact of it.

CONTENTS

PREFACE TO
THE REVISED EDITION

I had no idea when I wrote this book ten years ago that over 250,000 people would use it to improve their children's power to learn, and, indeed, to improve their own power to learn. I had no idea that it would be adopted by hundreds of teachers, dozens of high schools, and even a major university as a supplementary text. Nor that it would be translated into several languages, and sell tens of thousands of additional copies in Europe.

All this was a surprise—a monumental surprise. For all I was trying to do, when I wrote it, was teach one parent—you—how to help one child—your child—get out of school what he should get out of it.

The worst thing in life is to have talent and not be able to use it. To have brains and not be able to harness them. To have potential, that never becomes more than potential, because someone doesn't show you how to actualize it.

Kids are so smart they frighten you—if you give them a chance to show their smartness. Since this book was written, I have personally taught, and supervised the teaching, of a sufficient number of "slow learners." In the most dramatic case, these were children from the absolute bottom of the first and second grades in a Harlem public school. One of them was labelled as "brain-damaged." He, in three months, became the assistant teacher of the class, and that crippling label was removed forever. The others simply became "smart," because someone finally made learning make sense for them. And once you show a child—any child—how to make learning make sense, that child will just "gobble up" the world of ideas.

I have never met a stupid child. I have met many, many children who were labelled "stupid," who then went on to thrill me by creating their own sonnets, or philosophies, once they had been shown really how.

And there, I think, is the key. To show a child "how" is to show him everything. Because once he knows how to proceed—i.e., what is the first small, sensible step he should take, and then what is the second—he can then go on by himself to learn whatever it is he needs at that moment, or whatever it is he is interested in at that moment.

It is exactly as though you had given him a key that unlocks an infinite number of doors, each one of which contains either food or a treasure hidden behind it. The doors he has to open himself. And they will probably be different doors than you will choose. But once you give him the key, all the rest is simply a matter of choice.

Most of the human mind exists outside the human brain. It exists in books, in lectures, in research reports, in market analyses, in specialized publications, in complicated mathematical equations and a thousand other storage areas where words and symbols are piled up to increase the competence and power to survive of the human race. It is somewhat as if all this mass of information and wisdom were stored in a giant computer, and each one of us is a separate little terminal that feeds out of it. But to tap that central computer, we have to plug into it, and that plugging in is the ability to learn. Once we get plugged in, we are each as large and powerful as that huge computer. But, without being plugged in—without the ability to learn—we are very small and vulnerable indeed.

So we are reissuing this book. It reads well ten years after. It still accomplishes its basic goal—it teaches a child the fundamental, 1-2-3 steps of learning how to learn. It contains many of the tools your child needs. Therefore, I think it is of value to both you, and to him. I hand it on to you again, at this much later date, with the hope that it helps make your child what you know he or she can be.

Good luck with it. If you have any comments or suggestions, I would appreciate your letting me know.

—EUGENE M. SCHWARTZ

HOW TO DOUBLE
YOUR CHILD'S
GRADES
IN SCHOOL

INTRODUCTION

What Top Grades Really Mean to Your Child's Future.

Let me be brutally frank right at the start. In this modern, scientific, competitive world of ours, *your child's success or failure is molded before he or she is twelve, in the examination rooms of your public school.*

This all-important fact must be repeated over and over again: *No matter what the sex of your children—boy or girl —the entire quality of their future lives will be determined by their performance in school.*

By this I mean that the size of their income, the kind of person they will marry, the station they attain in life, even the satisfaction they get out of their spare-time activities—all will be decided by their ability to keep up with their classmates in school, or forge ahead of them.

Does this sound impossible? Then consider these cold, hard facts:

1. About ONE THIRD of your child's life will be spent in school. He or she will spend about 10,000 hours in elementary school, 6,000 hours in high school, and 6,000 hours or more in college.

2. Almost everything that happens to those children in school—in that character-forming first one third of their lives —will depend on their ability to master facts. On the basis of his performance in class, your boy, or girl, will be branded as slow or fast, as a leader or a follower, as someone to seek after or someone to leave behind.

3. And his progress through school, the amount of real

3

education he gets, will depend entirely on his grades. These grades will determine whether he is placed in a slow or fast group, whether he gets the best teachers or the worst, whether he will be allowed to take advanced subjects and foreign languages, whether he is to go into a college-preparatory class or be barred forever.

4. And it is a college education that is the great open door to the top futures of tomorrow. With college, your son will earn up to $250,000 more in his lifetime than he would earn if he is stopped in high school. With college, your daughter will meet the only men who can go places in her world of tomorrow—career men, who overwhelmingly marry girls they meet on their college campus.

5. But colleges are overcrowded to the point of explosion. Even today, every year a half million students take the Scholastic Aptitude Test to get into college. Even today, state universities demand high-school-grade averages of 88 per cent for boys and 91 per cent for girls, just to walk inside the doors.

6. And even higher grades are required for your children to earn scholarships, scholarships that can save you thousands of dollars on their college costs, get them into the institutions of their choice rather than a second-best compromise, and perhaps even mean the difference between going or not going to college at all.

This, then, is the effect top grades will have on your children by the time they are eighteen years old—ready to enter college.

These grades will determine their self-image and self-confidence, rate them with their teachers and their fellow students, open up or close forever dozens of special advantages, and finally, if you are wise, admit them to the brilliant world of the college campus.

But this entrée to college—this first real step upward—is only the beginning. For it is in college, and beyond, that the competition really stiffens. And the ability to master

*facts—to really understand what your child is doing—pays off
far beyond your fondest dreams.*

Consider these further facts:

7. Once he's in college, the kind of grades your child
gets there determines the kind of job he's offered when he
gets out. Even today, the country's largest blue-chip cor-
porations, when they are interviewing college graduates, set
their sights on the top 10 per cent of the class. Usually they
will not even interview anyone outside that select group.

8. And from the moment he graduates, the same sink-
or-swim story repeats itself, time and time again. At every
turning point in his career, your child will reap a fortune
from the priceless ability to absorb facts, master facts, put
facts to immediate use. Here are just a few of these pay-off
situations, where he wins or loses on the basis of his ability
to think:

9. When he takes any one of the thousand tests that are
now given in adult life. A licensing test for a profession or
trade. A graduate study test for an advanced degree that
will add extra thousands of dollars a year to his income. A
qualification test that could get him an appointment to
Annapolis or a civil-service job, or win him an Army or Navy
commission. Or simply the dozens of daily tests that enable
him to drive a car, own a boat, repair an airplane, build
himself a radio transmitter.

10. Plus, of course, the job-advancement tests that he
will face as much as once a year, every year, for the rest
of his life. Tests that determine his rate of progress, his
yearly pay scale, whether he'll be put on special managerial
staffs, be given expensive training to prepare him for a
better position, break ahead of the field, go forward as fast
as he really can. Even whether he'll be forced to retire too
early, or take a less demanding job, or continue on to the
top as before.

*All of it—his own self-confidence, his advancement in
school, his dollar-and-cents success in later life—depends*

overwhelmingly on his ability to master facts, his ability to squeeze every ounce of power out of his brain that Nature has built into it.

And that ability—today more than ever before—depends on YOU.

Is It Really That Hard to Get Top Grades? The Answer Is No.

Once—perhaps ten years ago—the facts I've listed above might have been considered a life sentence of failure for the child who was having trouble with his schoolwork, day after day.

Ten years ago, we might have believed that poor grades reflected a poor mind, that the student who did badly in class lacked either scholastic ability or intelligence.

We might have believed this ten years ago. But today we realize that it's a myth.

Again, let's look at the facts.

Given average ability, students who do badly in school do badly because no one has ever taught them to study efficiently.

Without the proper study techniques, it is perfectly possible for your child to get only HALF what he should get out of his lesson. Without the proper retention techniques, it is possible for him to remember only HALF of what he has understood. And without the proper test-taking techniques, it is possible for him to score only HALF the grade he could otherwise attain. We doom him, through our negligence, to struggling through school as a HALF-DOER.

Your child does not have to be brilliant to succeed either in school or life. The only thing separating an average child from a fruitful scholastic life is DIRECTION—the ability to get the best possible results out of his own efforts.

Given this direction, any child with average intelligence

can maintain a superior school average. Every year, students who know how to study get grades far beyond those that might be expected from their IQ ability level. The difference is TECHNIQUE, pure and simple.

Technique . . . Direction . . . Guidance . . . Method! These are the secrets of success in school. Not an IQ. Not "inborn ability." Not some mysterious hidden talent that enables a few gifted students to solve problems at a glance that other students would never be able to understand, no matter how hard they worked on them.

This idea is pure nonsense. The real difference between the top student and the mediocre student lies, not in ability, but in technique. And technique can be TAUGHT.

Because of this one simple fact—and because of the almost miraculous breakthroughs that have been achieved in the last few years in teaching children how to study—there is no longer any reason for any child to be forever catching up while his classmates are going forward, to suffer the gloom and discouragement of always being behind, to experience school as drudgery and disappointment, to be branded as dull or slow-minded, and to be known forever as a four-cylinder student in an eight-cylinder society.

Study is a skill, and it can be improved by practice like any other skill.

The ability to study can be improved drastically by learning a few simple techniques of studying scientifically.

And YOU can teach your child enough of these techniques in a single week to literally start him on the road to doubling his grades in school.

Here Is Exactly What This Book Will Do for You—and Your Child.

This is the purpose of this book. To teach you how to double your child's grades in school with the least effort, and in the shortest possible time.

I believe that next to loving your child this is the most important task you will ever be given as a parent. And next to love this is the greatest single gift you will ever give him.

But why YOU? Why should YOU have to teach him these skills? Why not his teacher, in school?

For another very simple reason—OVERCROWDING. Packed classrooms. Half-day students. Thirty children to a teacher. Not enough personal attention. Not enough explanation of difficult problems. Not enough individual drill.

Your child's teacher doesn't even have enough time to teach him all the facts he should know about his course, let alone teach him how to master these facts. YOU have to work as a team with that teacher, to make sure your child knows these priceless study techniques.

This is the conclusion my own son's principal and I came to, in his very first grade in school. There is nothing in this book that conflicts in any way with what your child is being taught in school.

Exactly the opposite. The techniques in this book are designed to make the learning of that school material twice as easy and twice as fast, to make the absorption and mastery of that material almost automatic, to greatly relieve the teacher's burden by sending your child to class PREPARED to absorb her facts.

And what will these techniques do for your child? Simply this:

1. They will destroy present study habits that make his learning unpleasant and burdensome, and replace them with new, simpler, and easier habits that turn study into a thrilling, soaring hour of achievement every time your child opens a book.

2. In other words, they will reduce effective study procedures to the habit level. They will make them *a part of your child*, so that he gets right down to the core of every lesson, automatically, the instant he opens his book.

3. Because of these new study habits, and sooner than

you dare expect today, your child's ability to learn and to perform will zoom, will reveal such a change that his teacher may actually call you to see what happened.

4. Study periods will shrink in time—sometimes actually in half—while the work turned out from them will double in quantity and quality.

5. And there will be no more forcing your child to study. Study will suddenly become a privilege rather than a punishment, because each new lesson will give him a new taste of success, a new thrill of understanding, a stronger and stronger realization that he can conquer knowledge and make it his own, day after day.

6. Therefore conduct in class will improve, as your child gets his satisfaction from achievement, from performance, rather than frustrated rebellion. He will make new friends, better friends, "achievers" like himself, boys and girls who are really going places in this modern scientific world of ours.

7. But, above all, he will be *happier*, because he is doing something he is successful at. And this is the number-one requirement for happiness in anything we do in life.

And what of his grades? What will happen to the marks he brings home—those magic percentage points that are the passports to college, scholarship, and the great world of achievement beyond? Simply this:

8. His grades will double. Let me be perfectly clear on this point. Your child's grades—if he applies these techniques—will actually double.

This means that if he is now getting a "C" in class, he will get a "B." If he is now getting a "B," he will get an "A." And if he is now getting a "D" or below, the results may be even more dramatic.

If your child is graded by a percentage-point system rather than letters, this doubling process will result in an improvement of about ten to fifteen points tacked on to his previous grades. Where he had 70 before, he may now reach

80 or even 85. Where he scored 80 before, he may go as high as 95.

This dramatic jump in grades, produced over and over again, in test after test, will put him in the advanced class he would have otherwise missed, will give him the ability to choose the college he wants, which might otherwise have barred him, may even bring in the scholarship you need to send him to the best school in the country.

Isn't this worth one week's pleasant reading right now, and a few minutes' checking a day while your child is forging ahead?

That's all it takes. All the equipment you need is right here. These simple rules apply to any child, at any level, in any grade.

To put them to work for YOUR CHILD—to carve out the life of success and achievement you want for YOUR CHILD—you start right here.

PART ONE

THE SIMPLE STRATEGY OF TOP GRADES

CHAPTER 1

HOW GOOD ARE YOUR CHILD'S STUDY HABITS TODAY?
TAKE THIS THREE-MINUTE TEST

Is your child living up to his or her full potential? Is your child squeezing out the absolute top grades that his inborn intelligence will give him?

In other words, are your child's present study habits helping him or hindering him? Is the power of his brain being harnessed from the very first minute he opens a book —or blocked every step of the way?

This three-minute check list will tell you right now. It is a quick, scientific run-down, not of your child's intelligence or ability, but of the results his present study habits are capable of giving him.

Simply observe your child studying for a single night. Then answer these questions with a yes or a no. In three brief minutes, every weak spot in your child's study pattern will be thrown into the spotlight. You'll see the road-blocks in his way, and you'll take your first step toward removing them.

Here they are. Answer them coldly and honestly.

DOES YOUR CHILD:
Have trouble finding studying materials? ——
Take hours to get himself going on his homework? ——
Find it hard to keep his mind on what he's studying? ——
Have trouble picking out the main points of the lesson he's reading? ——
Forget the next day what he read the night before? ——
Spend fruitless hours trying to figure out standard math problems? ——

Make the same mistakes over and over again? ——
Constantly come to you to solve his homework? ——
Have difficulty expressing his own thoughts on paper?
——

Imitate other children's reports and compositions, rather
than create his own? ——
Forget vocabulary words almost as fast as he learns
them? ——
Have a notebook that's a mess of illegible scribbles and
torn-up pages? ——
Never finish his work on time? ——
Cram desperately for tests? ——
Become sick with fear before tests? ——

How many questions did you answer with yes? If
there was even one, this book will be worth far more to
you and your child than the price you paid for it.

If you had four yes answers, then your child is losing
over 25 per cent of his brain power through sloppy study
habits. In other words, he is achieving at least 25 per cent
poorer grades than his inborn ability should give him. This
book will restore those lost percentage points.

And if you had eight or more yes answers, then your
child is in trouble; you can see it at a glance; and you—and
he—are in for one of the most dramatic and painless improve-
ment performances of your entire lives.

Save this test. Check your answers, in pen or pencil, on
this page. Refer back to each yes answer—to each weak point
—as you reach the section that covers it in this book.

Then, one week from now, when you've finished this
book, and you and your child have run through the methods
described in its pages—at that point take this test again.
Write down your new answers—one week from today—next
to the old.

The difference may actually take your breath away.
You can actually see your child grow, see his study habits

change in that first week, see him turn the corner to success.

And if there are any yes answers left at the end of that first week—or at the end of his first big test—then simply mark those weak points. Run over the procedures with him again. And repeat the test one month later.

You'll see those yes answers evaporate like water on a hot stove. And you'll see the results of those procedures—in black and white—on his next report card. *And on every single report card, in every single subject, that he brings home from that day on.*

NOTE: Throughout the remainder of this book, it will be simpler if I just refer to your child as "he," even though the child may be a girl. It's much too awkward to say "he or she" in every sentence. So with due apologies to all our beautiful little daughters, let's just sum them all up as "he." Thanks.

CHAPTER 2

OUR PLAN OF ATTACK FOR HIGHER GRADES OVERNIGHT—
WHAT YOU AND YOUR CHILDREN MUST DO

The Joseph Kennedys knew the secret. Perhaps that's why they produced so many outstanding men in a single generation of children.

In a cover article in *Time* magazine, in September, 1962, just before Ted Kennedy was elected United States Senator, the Kennedy method of raising leaders was described in detail. It went something like this:

The Kennedy children were taught how to win—and to be responsible for winning—from the time they could first read.

Every evening, when they came down to dinner, these children passed a bulletin board on their way to the table. On that board were posted the day's events. What had happened that day in politics, business, Europe, science, sports.

The children paused for a moment before that board— reading, absorbing, memorizing, thinking. For they knew that, when they reached the table, they would be questioned about every event posted on that board. They would have to remember every important detail on that board. They would have to retell every episode in their own words—with every fact and figure precisely correct.

And they would have to give their own opinion of why it had happened, and what would happen next. And they would have to defend that opinion against their brothers— and make that opinion stick.

Every night, the same priceless training. Five minutes a day to mold brilliance and leadership into growing children.

16

To give them these all-important gifts:

1. The ability to read quickly and surely, and understand every word they read.

2. The ability to pick out the important details from a mass of words, and burn them indelibly into their minds.

3. The ability to express their own thoughts in their own words, and to express them quickly, powerfully, and convincingly.

4. The ability to reason, to think logically, to fill in unstated facts, to detect lies and errors, to project present events into the future, to persuade others to accept their point of view.

These gifts were worth far more to the Kennedy children than the vast fortunes their father provided for them. And they were transmitted at no greater cost than five minutes a day of their parents' time and direction.

That same five minutes a day you can give to your children to build success into their future. And it is the only cost, of either time or money, that this book asks of you.

Here is the reason why:

THE THREE SIMPLE BUILDING BLOCKS OF SUCCESS

In the past few years, a great many parents have become confused. They have become so fascinated with social studies, physics, foreign languages, and the like, that they have forgotten how simple a good education really is.

A good education—a bedrock education—an education upon which your children will either succeed or fail for the rest of their lives—*consists of just three simple skills*:

The ability to read,

The ability to express thoughts in words, and

The ability to solve mathematical problems.

Reading, writing and arithmetic. The old-timers knew it. We've forgotten it; and we have to get back to it.

These are the foundation stones. Everything else, all the advanced subjects, depends on them. For example, if you can't understand what you read, you can't read science. If you can't express your own thoughts, you can't write good advertising copy. And if you can't solve simple problems in addition or subtraction, then you won't even be able to start on calculus or aerodynamics.

Everything your child does in his future grades, and in his future life, depends upon his ability to read, to write, and to figure. For the rest of his life, he'll be reading newspapers, memos, articles, and reports. For the rest of his life, he'll be writing letters, applications, recommendations, and progress reports. For the rest of his life, he'll be figuring grocery bills, installment charges, mortgage payments, and profit and loss.

If he can't read like an expert, write like an expert, and figure like an expert, then anything else you do for his mind will be wasted.

Therefore your fundamental task—the one great secret of building success into your child—is to make absolutely sure that that child is a "blooming genius" in reading, writing, and arithmetic.

And I mean *genius!* When we get through with that child of yours, we're going to have his classmates pop-eyed at his ability to read a printed page, to write a written report, to cut through a mathematical problem to its very heart.

Reading, writing, and arithmetic. You are going to make your child a master in each of these. And you are going to do it in five short minutes a day, using these three incredibly powerful tools:

> Enthusiasm,
> Praise,
> And a good, kind ear.

Here's how they combine to get your child off to a whizbang start—today.

WHAT YOUR CHILD READS MEANS NOTHING. IT'S WHAT HE CAN PUT TO USE THAT COUNTS.

Your primary job, then, is twofold. First, you must teach your child the scientific techniques of reading, writing, and arithmetic contained in this book.

And second, you must get your child to put them to use, to recite in front of you, so you can make absolutely sure he's got them right.

This is the one-two punch that knocks tough subjects into a cocked hat, that shoots grades up overnight. It's a combination of:

1. New scientific techniques of study,
2. Backed up by a daily parent check-up to see that your child's using them correctly.

In computer language, this checking-up process is called "feedback." Engineers know that it's not what you feed into a computer that counts; it's what that computer does with that information—what it "feeds back" to you—that counts. Some of that information can be lost, forgotten, or distorted. You have to ask for it again to make sure.

The same with your child. In every one of his subjects, for every day of his school career, what he reads means nothing. Words can simply pour in and out of his mind like water through a funnel. The only thing that counts is what sticks. How much he understands. How much he remembers. And how much he can put to immediate use.

Burn this fact into your mind. To learn any subject, mere reading is only the first step. *The complete, effective learning process is made up of these four steps:*

Reading,
Understanding,
Remembering, and
Reproducing, in his own thoughts and words.

This is the end goal you want for your child. Reproducing, putting to use, expressing in his own words, either on paper or in classroom recitation. (Or, in the case of mathematics, in solving new problems.)

This is what you are aiming at, the end result. If his learning process stops short of this goal, this effective self-expression, then your child is failing his study period. He is getting only half the benefit of his work.

You have to make sure that he gets it all. *You* have to check up on his work every single day. Here's how you do it:

THE FIVE-MINUTE ACHIEVEMENT CHECK ON YOUR CHILD'S DAILY WORK

Starting today, and continuing for every day of your child's school career, do this:

Both parents should spend at least five minutes a day with their child and his homework. The time of day is unimportant; but you must be able to give that time completely to your child, in full concentration upon his problems, with no interruptions and no sense of being hurried.

For these few minutes each day, nothing in the world matters but your child and his homework.

This is a recitation period, a discussion period, and eventually a "show-off" period. It should have the following schedule, and you should run through the entire schedule, in the exact order given, each day.

1. Examine the work he is going to turn in to class next morning. See that it is neat and clean.

2. See that it has no misspelled words.

3. Question what is not clear to you, and have him explain it to you till you are sure he understands it.

4. Hear his memory work.

5. Check his arithmetic work for neatness and cleanness only.

6. Check his assignment book to see that he has completed all his homework.

7. Now check the work he has received back from the

teacher. If it has errors on it, turn the paper over and ask him to rework the problems on its back till he gets the correct answers. Every error must be redone correctly the same day it is handed back to him.

You have now completed the Achievement Check. At the beginning it will take more than five minutes. But soon your child will understand what you expect of him. His work will improve. He will be prepared for the check. And you will zip through it with him with perhaps the warmest glow of pride you have known in years.

In every case, if his work does not meet your standards, then he must do it over again. And submit it again, and again, until it is right.

But your criticism of his work must be objective, calm, sympathetic. There must be no punishment, no raised voices, no downgrading. You are there to help him, and not humiliate him. You must make it perfectly clear at every session that you know that he can do the job, that these are only temporary set-backs, that you are looking forward to the day, with complete confidence, when your only reaction to his work will be undiminished praise.

And when that day comes, and for every tiny victory of his on the way to that day, *make sure above all that you are lavish with that praise.*

THE MOST POWERFUL WEAPON YOU HAVE TO ENCOURAGE TOP GRADES FROM YOUR CHILD.

Let me emphasize this fact again:

Praise makes winners.

Encouragement—not criticism—builds success into those you are trying to help.

Enthusiasm is the magic ingredient that makes people perform miracles, that brings home results far beyond your fondest dreams.

Just visualize your child's world for a moment. Realize

that every arithmetic paper graded 100 is as important to him as is a salary raise to you. Every word spelled correctly is as thrilling to him as is a meal perfectly prepared to you.

It takes as much torment and effort for your child to learn to multiply two numbers together as it does for you to prepare an entire merchandising campaign, or strip down and put together a complete engine, or to plan and put into execution a city-wide charity drive for your neighborhood church.

The effort is exactly the same. And the feeling of accomplishment and pride is also exactly the same. Therefore, when such accomplishment occurs—no matter how tiny it may seem to you—view it through your child's eyes and reward him accordingly.

In other words, make a large-scale fuss about very small accomplishments. And soon those accomplishments will grow very large indeed.

Always remember, your job is not only to implant skill in your child, but self-confidence as well. And self-confidence comes from only one source—admiration and praise. Accomplishment must be rewarded.

In summary:

Your child's entire education rests on his mastery of three bedrock skills:

> Reading,
> Writing, and
> Mathematics.

The purpose of this book is to help you improve those skills to the point of near-perfection. This is done in two ways:

1. By teaching your child new scientific techniques of learning how to learn; and

2. By checking back on your child's work every day, to make sure he has understood these techniques and put them to use.

The basic procedure is therefore this. All schoolwork papers—coming and going—must be brought to your attention and gone over carefully. All mistakes must be corrected, neatness praised, success rewarded.

Through this simple procedure, your child will learn a respect for, and a striving toward, that most magic of all words—excellence.

We are striving in this book for excellence in your child.

And we begin by teaching him a few simple tricks of organization, to help him get twice as much done in half the time he spends today.

CHAPTER 3

ORGANIZATION. HOW TO GET TWICE AS MUCH DONE IN HALF THE TIME

Most school children waste at least half their study time, because no one has ever shown them how to organize their work.

This is the purpose of this chapter—to cut the waste out of your child's study, and make sure he gets a full minute's results for every minute he spends with his books.

WHAT IS ORGANIZATION?

Organization is simply *planned direction*. It is a procedure. A system. A planned schedule of events or tasks, one after the other, that gets something done in the shortest possible time, with the least amount of waste.

It is doing the right thing at the right time. And not wasting your time doing the wrong thing.

In regard to your child's schoolwork, therefore, organization is basically a way of sitting down at a desk,

finding out what has to be done,

opening the right book to the right page to do it,

starting to do it at the beginning.

learning it step by step,

knowing when it is finished and when it is right,

and then remembering what it is he has done, how he has done it, and what use he can put it to tomorrow.

Without such a definite step-by-step plan of attack, your child must waste time. Because he will not get down to work immediately. He will not be sure exactly what it is he is supposed to learn. He will wander aimlessly till he stumbles on it. And then he may lose it again, or waste time reading on after he has learned it, or forget it before he gets to class the next day.

Therefore the most beautiful thing about organization is that it is *far simpler and far easier* than what he is doing today. It not only gives him higher grades—instantly—but it does it with far less study time.

And it's so easy to put into practice. All the organization he needs can be broken down into two simple formulas:

1. Getting down to work; and
2. Doing the work right.

Let's look at each of them in turn.

NO MORE CRISES. NO MORE FEAR.

Any subject becomes easy if you organize it on a long-term basis, day by day, lesson by lesson, step by step. Constant, daily study periods, therefore, are the first magic key to success.

The first step in organizing your child's study habits is to set up a daily work schedule for him, and make sure you both stick to it.

There is just no substitute for regular daily study—for a certain amount of time spent daily on each subject. Life as a student becomes incredibly easy if he maintains a steady pace from start to finish of the school year. Then there are no sudden pressures to get things done. No near-hysteria about deadlines. No tensions and anxieties in class.

With a daily work schedule, religiously enforced, all these crises are miraculously replaced by the wonderfully secure feeling of being adequately prepared. Which, in turn, leads to a steady, comforting flow of high marks.

Let's look at such a daily schedule, and see how simple it is to set up, and how easy it is to follow.

YOUR CHILD'S DAILY ACHIEVEMENT SCHEDULE

Monday through Friday:
7:00 A.M.—Get-up time.
7:05-7:30—Wash, dress, shine shoes.
7:30-7:45—Breakfast.
7:45-8:00—Help around the house.
8:00-8:10—Final preparation for school.
8:10-8:30—Going to school.
8:30-8:45—Pre-school talk with friends.
8:45-2:45—Regular class schedule.
2:45-3:15—Going home from school.
3:15-5:15—Recreation, practice, and so on.
5:15-5:45—Help in house and wash up.
5:45-6:30—Dinner.
6:30-6:45—Help with clean-up.
6:45-7:00—Make ready for study time—get all equipment together.
7:00-8:00—Study hour.
8:00-8:05—Parent check on homework.
8:05-9:00—Watch TV, read, relax.
9:00-9:15—Prepare for bed.
9:15-7:00—Sleep.

Saturday—a free day.
Sunday—a free day.

The exact details in this schedule are, of course, merely suggestions. Your own family activities may dictate different dinner hours, relaxation breaks, parent checks, and so on. And, of course, as your child enters high school, and beyond, the study period will have to be lengthened to two hours or more each night.

But the important points are clear. Every day—every single day—there must be at least one hour for study and five minutes for recitation. Without exception. Without excuse. Without delay.

This study period is essential to your child's career. It

is as vital to his future as is your work to yours. *And it must start at exactly the same time each night. It must be entered into without delay. And it must be followed by a careful, concentrated check before that child can close his books and go on to something else.*

Let's take a closer look at that daily study period and see how we can make it produce twice the results for your child.

TIPS THAT DOUBLE THE VALUE OF EACH STUDY HOUR

1. Your child will not do top work in his study period unless you make that study period as important to you as it is to him. This means:

2. He must have a definite place to study. It must be *his* place. The same place each night. With no one else having any claim to it for that hour.

3. It must be comfortable and bright. With the physical equipment he needs to read and write permanently stored there, instantly at hand when he wants to use it.

4. There must be no distractions for that hour. This means, ideally, his own room with the door closed. No radio or TV. No interruptions. No friends working with him. No phone calls permitted for any reason. When he gets down to work, he stays at work till he's finished.

If he does not have his own room, then he must be given the exclusive use of one room for that hour. This means no other members of the family with him. No conversations near by, no rustle of newspapers. He needs silence to concentrate. And you have to make whatever sacrifices are necessary to give it to him.

5. But this ruling out of distractions goes one step further. It also means that he has with him, at study time, only the equipment he needs and nothing more. No unnecessary books. No newspapers. No pretty pictures on the wall to draw away his attention. Study is business—all business.

6. Make sure he starts his lessons at the same exact moment every day. A five-minute delay can kill an entire study period. The phone conversation is cut off, and he's at his desk at the precise moment he's scheduled to be there.

7. You are setting up a *routine*. A constant, daily psychological readiness to study. An automatic ability to concentrate that can only come from getting down to work at the same time, in the same spot, every day. Once this routine is established, waste motion is eliminated and work flashes by. At the end of that period, when you are ready to review that work, you will be delighted at the quantity and quality of it.

In summary:

Organization is planned direction. It is the ability of your child to

1. Get down to work without waste motion, and
2. Get the work done right.

In this chapter we have seen that organization makes even the hardest subjects easy by attacking them on a day-after-day basis.

In order to do this, a definite study hour must be set aside for your child every day, at exactly the same time, in exactly the same spot, with exactly the same equipment.

Once this routine is established, getting down to work becomes instant and automatic. Your child is ready to slash into his work without a second's waste motion.

Now let's teach him the second part of organization: How to fill up that study period with achievement. How to do that work right.

We'll start with the basic art of reading. How to cut through it in half his present time, with absolute understanding of every word he reads.

PART TWO

DIGGING OUT THE FACTS—READING

CHAPTER 4

The first requirement to be a good reader is *mastery of words*.

As your child reads, as he listens, as he gains information from any source whatever, *he learns new words*.

This word learning is one of the most important parts of his education. For words are the tools of thought. Mental tools that make thought far easier, far more exact, far more powerful in solving the problems he will encounter in later life.

The more words he learns, the more mental tools he has to work with. The purpose of this chapter is to show you how to help him master these tools.

HOW TO BUILD WORD POWER INTO YOUR CHILD FROM THE VERY FIRST GRADE

What is the proper age to actively teach your child new words—to deliberately expand his vocabulary? At the very latest, by the time he is in the first grade. It is so easy to do, and so much fun, that it makes one of the most entertaining and profitable parent-and-child games ever invented. Here's how it goes:

One night, at the dinner table, take a sentence out of his first reader. For example: "Ralph and Sue could not climb the green tree." Take a phrase out of that sentence, for example, "the green tree."

And then begin to explore other "tree" words with the child. Open up whole new realms of existence for him,

31

simply by substituting one word for another, like this:

You tell him this kind of story:

"Are there many green *trees* in your city block? Of course not.

"Then let's take a mental trip outside the city to the *fields* where you and your friends can run and play.

"Just beyond those fields is the edge of a *wood*, with many trees, and that wood is also called a *grove*.

"If the wood is thick enough and reaches far enough, so that we might easily get lost in it if we go too far, we call it a *forest*.

"And if it is still larger yet, and covers hills and valleys and mountains and lakes, then it is a *wilderness*.

"And, finally, if it is in the South, where it is very warm, and the trees are thick and soggy, and there are strange and dangerous animals lurking everywhere, it is a *jungle*, and we go into it only with a gun."

So you see how even so simple a word as *tree*, to children who are no older than five or six, can grow in pictures and feelings. Can make up wonderful new worlds of adventure. Can make your child's storehouse of words expand and expand.

But how many of these new words has he retained? Now you find out by asking him questions like these:

"What is a *grove*?"

"If a forest is so big that it covers hills and valleys and mountains and lakes, what is it called?"

"Where are *jungles* found?"

And so on, until each of these new words becomes second nature to him, until you can fairly see his vocabulary stretch and grow before your very eyes.

HOW TO MAKE HIS RECITATIONS SPARKLE

Later, when he becomes eight or nine years old, you make the game still more interesting. Now it becomes the

Change-the-Word Game—a search for substitute words in a story, to see what magic changes he can make when he fits them in.

For example, take the magnificent line from the Old Testament: "When they were in the field, Cain rose up against Abel and slew him." What would happen if we changed the key words in this sentence? Would we make the sentence better? Would we add or subtract meaning? Ask your child to try it and see.

Perhaps the two of you will replace "rose up" with such words as *conspired against, blindly hated, treacherously attacked*.

Perhaps you will replace "slew" with such words as *killed, murdered, butchered, assassinated*.

Which of these new words is the most exciting? Which carries the thought best?

As you play on, your child learns to search for exactly the right word to project the color and meaning of what he wants to say. He feels at home with all kinds of words—small and large, simple and exotic. He adds drama and depth to everything he says or writes. And you see the difference almost immediately in his grades.

HOW TO TEACH HIM TO IDENTIFY STRANGE WORDS, WITHOUT LOOKING THEM UP

Still later, at ten or eleven, your child will be ready to play the most thrilling and profitable game of all—learning how words are built. Recognizing the meaning of new words without having to interrupt his reading to look them up.

This also can be made an adventure in learning, if you follow this simple, two-step plan:

First of all, show your child that all words are built up, part by part, just as a model airplane is.

Words, however, are much more simple. They have just these three basic parts:

1.   They have a *root* or *stem*, which tells us the basic meaning, such as "go."

2.   Then there is the *front part* or *prefix*, which adds another meaning to the root word, such as "out" plus "go" equals "outgo."

3.   And then there is the *end part* or *suffix*, which gives us still another meaning. For example, "ing," which rounds out our word to give us "out" plus "go" plus "ing" to add up to "outgoing."

Thus we can build one big word out of three small ones. And this gives us a brand-new word, which is much easier to remember, takes far less space to write, and actually gives us a brand-new meaning that we wouldn't have had with the three smaller words at all.

This is the way language grows. By taking two or three small words, and building a new word out of them. And, by doing it, giving us new meanings to solve new problems.

There are three basic building blocks, then, to build new words—the *root*, the *front part*, and the *end part*.

Some words have only the root, like *hear*. Other words have only the root and the end part, like *hearing*. Still others have only the root and a front part, like *unheard*. And still others have all three parts, like *unhearing*.

Now, how does this knowledge help your child to recognize strange words without looking them up? In a very simple way:

Most big words that he doesn't recognize are actually made up of smaller words, in exactly the manner we have just described. They are made up of the same three basic building blocks we've just examined.

However, most of these smaller word parts are in Latin, for the very simple reason that Latin was the ancient language that was the parent of our own English language.

Therefore, in order to work out the meaning of a strange word the first time he sees it, all he has to do is learn these Latin word parts, and see how they fit together to make new words.

THE MOST PROFITABLE WORD
GAME HE WILL EVER PLAY

Listed below are some of the most common Latin and Greek word parts in our language. It has been said that from a mere twelve of these parts, we have built over 2,500 English words. *No wonder it pays your child such incredible dividends to learn one or two of them every night.*

Let's start with the most common *front parts.* Here's the *front part* itself, what it means, and a common English word that uses it. Notice how easy the word is to understand at a glance, once you know the meaning of the *front part.*

FRONT PART	MEANING	COMMON WORD
a, au	not, without	atypical
ab, abs	to free from	absolve
ad	to	adhere
am, amb, ambi	about, around, both	ambiguous
amphi	both, around	amphibious
ante	before	anteroom
ant, anth, anti	opposed to	anti-labor
arch, archi	chief, principal	archbishop
aut, auth, auto	self	automatic
bi, bis	two, double	biennial
caco	bad, ill	cacophonous
cata	down, complete	catalogue
circum	around	circumference
cis	on this side of	cisatlantic
col, com, con, cor	jointly	combine
contra, contro	against	contradict
counter	in opposition to	counteract
de	from, down, completely	deduce
di, dis	away from	dismiss
dia	between	dialogue
en	in, into	energetic

FRONT PART	MEANING	COMMON WORD
ep, eph, epi	upon, on, over	epitaph
equi	equal	equidistant
eu	well, good	euphony
ex, e	out	exit
extra	beyond, outside of	extraordinary
hetero	another, different	heterogeneous
hyper	over	hypercritical
hypo	under, below	hypodermic
i, il, im, in, ir, ig	not	inept
inter	between	interstate
intra	within	intrastate
intro	place before	introduce
mal, male	bad	malpractice
meta	after, change	metaphor
mis	wrong	mislabel
miso	hatred of	misogyny
mono	one, alone	monologue
multi	many	multiply
neo	new	neophyte
non	not	nonsense
ob	against	obstruct
ortho	correct, right	orthoptic
pan	all	panacea
para	beside	parallel
per	through	permit
peri	around	perimeter
poly	many	polygon
post	after	postscript
pre	before	prejudge
pro	before	pronoun
proto	first	protocol
pseudo	false, fictitious	pseudopod
psycho	relating to mind or soul	psychology
re, red	back, again	reincarnation
retro	back, backward	retrospect

FRONT PART	MEANING	COMMON WORD
se, sed	away, aside, apart	secede
semi	half	semi-circle
sub	under	submarine
super	above	superabundant
syn, sy	together	syntax
trans, tra	through, across	transport
tri	three	triangle
ultra	excessive	ultra-modest
un, uni	one	uniform
vice	in place of	vice versa

Now for END PARTS. Notice how they, too, add to the meaning of every word they touch.

END PART	MEANING	COMMON WORD
able, ible	above to be	believable
age	state	marriage
al	belonging to	constitutional
an, ave	belonging to	Georgian
an, ain	a member of	Republican
ance	quality	tolerance
ancy, ency	quality or state of	clemency
ant, ent	one who does	servant
ar	relating to	angular
ard, art	one who does	coward
ary	engaged in	secretary
ate	to make	animate
ation	the act of	dedication
cy	practice of	democracy
dom	state of	martydom
ee	one who receives	assignee
eer	one who is engaged in	volunteer
en	to make	moisten
ern	belonging to	western

END PART	MEANING	COMMON WORD
er	one who does	miner
er	belonging	Marylander
ery	occupation	surgery
esque	like, style of	statuesque
ferous	bearing, giving	auriferous
fold	number	twofold
ful	full of	resentful
gram	a writing	telegram
graph	a writing	autograph
hood	state of	brotherhood
ial	pertaining to	editorial
ic, ical	resembling	fantastic
ice	act, quality	justice
ify	to make	gratify
il, ile	capable of being	versatile
ine	of the nature of	canine
ion	the act of	decision
ious	full of	ambitious
ish	characteristic of	bookish
ism	state of	fascism
ist	one who practices	communist
ity	quality of	acidity
ive	tending to	abusive
ize	to follow an action	economize
less	lacking	useless
ling, long	showing direction	headlong
logy	science of	theology
ly	having qualities of	friendly
ment	act or process of	investment
ness	a quality	happiness
ogy	study of	geology
or	one who does	tailor
ory	of	prohibitory
ose	containing	verbose
ous	full of	mountainous

END PART	MEANING	COMMON WORD
ry	practice of	dentistry
sion	the act of	ascension
tion	the act of	inspection
trix	feminine agent	executrix
tude	state of	rectitude
ty	practice of	fidelity
ure	act of	rapture
vorous	feeding on	carnivorous
ward	direction of	eastward
wise	way of	clockwise
wright	maker	playwright
y, ey	pertaining to	smoky

Now the *root words* themselves. There are, of course, hundreds of them. All we can do is list some of the most common here. If your child wishes to learn more of them, he can easily find them in any good book on word building.

Again, notice how seemingly hard words become a cinch to understand when your child recognizes their word parts. And also notice how the *front* and *end parts* also build up the meaning of each word.

ROOT WORD	MEANING	COMMON WORD
acer, acr	sharp	acerbity
ag, act, ig	carry on	agency
ali	nourish	alimentary
ali, allo, alle	other	alias
alter	another	alter
alt	high	altitude
ambul	walk	amble
am, em	friend	amicable
amo, ama	love	amorous
anim	life	animation

ROOT WORD	MEANING	COMMON WORD
annu, enni	year	annual
anthrop	man	anthropology
appe	a call upon	appeal
aqua, aque	water	aquatic
arbiter	a judge	arbitration
art	art	artistic
ast, astr	star	astrology
audi, aur, aus	hear	audible
bell	hostile	rebellious
bible	book	bibliography
bio	life	biology
brevi	short	abbreviate
cad, cas, cid	fall	cadence
cam, chamb	room	chamber
camp, champ	country	campus
cant, chant, cent	sing	cantate
ced, ceed, cess	go	recede
celer	speed	accelerate
cent	hundred	century
chief, cap	head	captain
cap, capt	take, seize	capture
chrom, chromo, chroma	color	panchromatic
chron, chrono	time	synchronize
cide, cis, cise	cut, kill	suicide, scissors
cit	arouse	excite
civ, civi	citizen	civic
clam, claim	shout	clamor
clud, cluse	close, shut off	exclude
cline	bend	recline
coc, coct	cook	concoct
col, cul	till	cultivate
cor, cord	hear	accord
corp, corps, corpor	body	corporation

ROOT WORD	MEANING	COMMON WORD
cras	tomorrow	procrastinate
cred, creed	believe	incredible
crea	create	creation
cresc, crue, cret, crete	grow	increase
crux, cruc	a cross	crucifix
crypt	hide	cryptogram
culp	guilt	culpable
cur, course	to run	concurrent
cur, cura	care	curate
cycl	wheel	cycle
deca, deci	ten	decade
dem, demo	people	democracy
dens	thick	dense
derm	skin	epidermis
dexter	right-handed	dexterity
di, dia	day	diary
dic, dict	speak	dictate
dign	worthy	dignitary
doc, doct	teach	doctrine
dom	master	dominate
dom	house	domestic
dorm	sleep	dormitory
du	two	duet
dur	hard, lasting	durable
duc, duct	lead	educate
dynam	power	dynamic
err	wander, go astray	errant
erg	work	energy
ego	I	egotist
fac	do	factory
fer	carry	transfer
ferv	boil	fervent
fid	faith, trust	fidelity
fil	son	filiate

ROOT WORD	MEANING	COMMON WORD
fin	limit	final
firm	strengthen	affirm
flex, flect	bend	flexible
flu, flux	flow	fluent
fort	strong	fortress
found, fuse, fund	pour	refund
fract, frang	break	fragile
frater	brother	fraternity
fug	flee	fugitive
gam	marriage	bigamist
go	earth	geography
gen	birth	gender
gest, ger	carry, bear	gestation
gov, gub	govern, rule	government
grad, gress	walk, go	progress
grand	great	grandeur
graph	write	autograph
grat	pleasing, agreeable	gratitude
grav	heavy	gravity
greg	crowd	congregate
hab, hib	have, hold	habit
homos	same	homonym
hydr	water	hydrant
ject	throw	reject
jud	right	judgment
junct, jug	join	junction
juven	young	juvenile
labor	toil, work	laboratory
laud	praise	laudatory
lav	wash, clean	lavatory
leg, lig, lect	read, choose	legible
leg	law	legislature
lib	book	library
liber	free	liberty
lig	bind	oblige

ROOT WORD	MEANING	COMMON WORD
liter	letter	literal
loc	place	location
locu, loqu	speak, talk	elocution
log	word	dialogue
luc, lum	light	illuminate
lud, lus	play	allude
magn	great	magnify
mand	order	mandate
man, manu	hand	manual
mar, mari	sea	maritime
mater, matr	mother	maternal
matur	ripe	mature
med	middle	median
men, ment	mind	demented
mens, mest	month	semester
merg	dip	submerge
meter	measure	diameter
mis, mit	send	permit
mon	advise	admonish
morph	shape	amorphous
mor, mort	death	mortal
mov, mot, mob	move	remove
mut	change	mutant
nasc, nat	born	nativity
nihil	nothing	annihilate
nom, nomin	name	nominate
nov	new	novice
nym	name	pseudonym
oper, opus	work	operator
path	feeling	sympathy
pater, patr	father	paternal
parl	talk	parliament
pars, part	a part	partner
ped, pod	foot	pedal
pel, puls	drive	impulse

ROOT WORD	MEANING	COMMON WORD
pend, pens	hang, weigh	impending
pet	seek, ask	petition
pet, petr	rock	petrify
omni	all	omnibus
phil	love	philosophy
phobia	fear	hydrophobia
phon	sound	telephone
plic	twist	complicate
poli	city, state	political
port	carry	portable
pon, pos	put, place	exponent
pot	power	potentate
prim	first	primary
pris, prehen	seize, grasp	apprehend
prob	test	probation
put	think	compute
pyr	fire	pyromaniac
rog	question	interrogation
reg, rec	direct	direct
rupt	break	rupture
sci, scio	know	conscience
scop	watch	telescope
scrib, script	write	describe
seg, sect	cut	section
sed, ses, sid	seat	session
sens, sent	feel	sentiment
sequ, secu, sue	follow	sequence
sign	sign, mark	designate
sol	alone	solitude
solv, solu	loosen, free	absolve
somin	sleep	insomnia
soph	wise, wisdom	sophomore
spec, spect, spic	look, see	spectacle
spir, spirit	breathe	aspire
spond	promise	despond

ROOT WORD	MEANING	COMMON WORD
sta, sti, sist	stand	circumstance
stead	place	steadfast
strict	bind	district
stru	build	structure
tact ting	touch	tactile
tail	cut	crutail
tang	touch	tangible
tend	extend	extend
tena, tain	hold	detain
tent, tempt	try	attempt
term	end, limit	terminal
terr, ter	earth	inter
tele	afar	telescope
theo	God	Theology
therm	heat	thermometer
thesis	setting, statement	thesis
tor, tort	twist	distort
tract	draw	tractor
trib	pay, grant	tribute
typ	model	typical
umbr	shadow	umbrella
urb	city	urban
val	strength	validity
ven, vent	come	convene
ver	true	veracity
vert, vers, verse	turn	divert
via, voy, vio	way	convey
vinc, vict	conquer	victor
vir	man	virile
voc	call	vocation
vol	wish	voluntary
volu, volv, volt	turn, roll	involve
zoo	animal	zoology

And, of course, many more. Your child should have a Word Part page in the back of his notebook. Every time he discovers a new word part, and learns its meaning, he should immediately write it down on this page for permanent reference. And, at the same time, he should immediately see how many different words he can find that use this part to build their meaning. This is easily one of the most fascinating and profitable word games he will ever play.

TWO DICTIONARIES EVERY CHILD SHOULD OWN

To look up these word parts, and to give him the meaning of every new word he should come across in his home studies, your child should have his own dictionary. This can be any of the good pocket dictionaries on the market until he reaches senior high school or college. And then it should be a college dictionary. It will be one of the most-used books in his entire library.

In addition to this personally owned reference dictionary, your child should build up a special technical dictionary for every course he studies. In every new course, especially in his high school and college years, he will have to master the *fundamental vocabulary* for that course.

For example, even in his grammar, he will have to know the meaning of *noun, pronoun, verb, adjective, adverb, preposition, participle, gerund, declension,* and dozens more.

Special words like these are often defined only once in a textbook—the first time they are introduced—and then used over and over again throughout the textbook without being defined again. Often your child will forget their meaning in the interval, and find that he is hopelessly lost in an advanced lesson.

This can easily be avoided by having him set up a Vocabulary Page in the back of each course section of his notebook. Here, each time he encounters a new word, he simply writes it down on this page, along with its precise definition. Then, when he comes across it again in his reading, he can simply look it up on his Vocabulary Page without loss of time or motion.

Remember, your child cannot understand a lesson unless he completely understands the meaning of every word in that lesson.

In summary:

Words are incredibly powerful mental tools that help your child solve problems. It has been found that the more successful the man, the larger his vocabulary.

Therefore you must help your child master the words he will need for success. This can be easily done, in these three ways:

1. By helping him develop the habit of searching for the exact right word. To enlarge his vocabulary to give color and power to every sentence he speaks or writes.

2. By teaching him the Latin and Greek word parts that make up our modern English language, and thus enable him to recognize hundreds of strange new words at a glance, without having to interrupt his reading to look them up immediately in a dictionary.

3. By having him build his own personal Fundamental Vocabulary Dictionary for every course he studies. Thus he will gain a complete mastery of the language of that course, gain a deeper understanding of its way of thought, and cut hours of study time from the effort it takes him to master it.

We now put these newly learned words to use in your child's reading and writing. We begin with his reading.

CHAPTER 5

HOW TO BECOME A MASTER READER
IN THREE EASY STEPS

The basic, fundamental skill required for all education is reading.

The ability of your child to study effectively, to get top grades in any subject, depends almost entirely on his ability to read thoroughly and with understanding. On his ability to pull facts out of a printed page and make them his own.

Even in mathematics, your child must first read the instructions and then understand precisely what he is to do to solve each of the problems.

If he cannot do this, if he cannot read any assignment with complete confidence and understanding, then he will go through the rest of his school life suffering from these two crippling handicaps:

1. He will be forever doing unnecessary work. Every assignment will become doubly difficult—read over and over again two or more times, with each sentence painfully spelled out and only partially understood. And

2. He will be forever making unnecessary mistakes. Teachers acknowledge that almost as many errors are made in homework and tests *through sheer misreading or misunderstanding of instructions alone as through lack of knowledge.*

Why burden him for the rest of his life with this double waste? Especially when effective reading—active, aggressive reading that tears knowledge out of the printed page and burns it into your child's memory for good—is far easier and far faster than the "spell-along" reading most children do today.

Here's why.

GOOD READING IS FAR MORE THAN MERELY RECOGNIZING WORDS.

We will assume in this book that your child already reads. In other words, that he can take the letters c-a-t and put them together to form the word "cat." And that he can take several such words, and read them in the sentence, "The cat chases the mouse."

This, really, is what we usually mean when we speak of the activity "reading." That your child can mechanically scan a printed page and put the words together from that page to form sentences.

In turn, this mechanical reading, by some magic process, is supposed to put knowledge in your child's mind. According to this theory, once he has read a sentence, or a series of sentences, the thought contained in them is supposed to automatically be transferred into his memory.

This is nonsense. Absolute nonsense. Every parent, at one time or another, has seen his child read an entire page, and then not be able to remember a single fact from it five minutes later.

Mere mechanical reading is not enough. Passive reading is not enough. The ability to run your eye over a printed page—to make words out of the print on that page and put them together into sentences—*is only the beginning of Effective Reading.*

Effective Reading is far more than this.

Effective Reading goes one step beyond mere words.

Effective Reading is the art of taking those words, and boiling them down into THOUGHTS. Of boiling down dozens, and even hundreds, of those words into ONE VITAL THOUGHT.

Of searching for the "guts" of an assignment—the two or three really important thoughts that it contains—and separating them from all the waste words and unnecessary details that surround them.

And then burning those few vital thoughts into your memory, so you can never forget them.

GOOD READING IS A SEARCH. A SEARCH FOR BIG IDEAS.

Let me repeat these all-important facts. Your child must be trained, not merely to read for words, but for *central thoughts*.

He must be taught that good reading is an active, aggressive search that has these three steps:

1. Locating a main idea in the mass of words that contain it.

2. Separating that idea from its unnecessary details. And

3. Boiling that idea down into a few easily remembered words.

Your child becomes a good reader, therefore, only when he masters this technique of searching and boiling down. Searching and boiling down. Searching and boiling down.

Till he has taken the entire assignment—hundreds upon hundreds of words, sentences, and paragraphs—and reduced them to a few vital thoughts that contain the meaning of them all, that sum up the meaning of them all.

And that can be burned into his memory forever in a few short moments. Ready to be put to use—to solve new problems or to answer questions in an examination—the very instant he needs them.

THIS IS A NEW WAY TO READ. TWICE AS FAST. FIVE TIMES AS EFFECTIVE.

The rest of this section will be devoted to teaching your child to read this new way. It is surprisingly easy to learn.

And it is far easier, and far faster, than his present method.

Let me outline right now what each of the following chapters is going to teach your child.

There are three easy steps to this new reading process. Each of the next three chapters explains one of them.

Chapters 6 to 8 show your child how to set up the search for big ideas. How to glance over his assignment, in one or two short minutes, and locate each of its important thoughts, *before* he begins to read.

Chapter 9 shows him how to Power-Read. How to flash through page after page, pulling out and marking down those important thoughts, merely glancing over their unnecessary details, and finishing with the assignment in half the time it has taken him before.

Chapter 10 shows him how to boil these vital thoughts down into a few words, and burn them into his memory with the very same action.

And Chapter 11 shows him how to use the same three-step technique in class, when he is listening to a lecture. It enables him to understand and remember what he *hears* equally well with what he *reads*.

When your child has finished this section, and put its simple methods to use, he will be a confident, accomplished reader. He will be able to read any assignment that is given to him, easily, swiftly, and without fear. He will understand each word he reads the instant he reads it. And he will remember the vital points of everything he reads and be able to put them to immediate use.

In summary:

Good reading is far more than merely recognizing the meaning of words.

Good reading is an active, aggressive search for the *major thoughts* that are contained in these words.

This search has three steps:

1. Locating the main ideas.
2. Separating them from their unnecessary details. And
3. Boiling them down into a few words that can be easily memorized.

Now let's put these three steps into action. Let's examine each of these techniques in detail, along with concrete examples of what they will accomplish for your child.

CHAPTER 6

HOW TO PRE-READ A LESSON—
UNDERSTAND IT BEFORE YOU READ

Let us suppose that your child is given a reading assignment in school. For example, he is told to read Chapter 6 in his history book on the Civil War. Or the next five pages on fractions in his arithmetic book. Or perhaps even a complete book report on *The Red Badge of Courage* by Stephen Crane.

He takes the book home. He sits down at his desk at the exact moment his evening study hour begins. And he opens the book to the page assigned.

What does he do now?

If he simply begins to read the first words he sees—if he plunges right into that text without making any further preparation—then he is making a crucial mistake that will cost him hours of waste effort every week, and that may cause him to miss the entire point of each lesson.

No one—no matter how bright—can really understand an assignment by simply beginning to read it word after word. It's like trying to go on a car trip by simply driving on to the first highway you see, without getting directions or looking at a road map.

Your child's first job in reading is to get those directions. To build himself that road map. To know exactly what he wants to get out of that lesson. And where it's located.

To do this, he *pre-reads* that lesson. He glances over that lesson from beginning to end—before he starts to read it. And he picks out the following information:

1. What's the main theme of this lesson? (For example, the Civil War.)

2. How much information does this lesson cover? (The period from 1861 to 1864.)

3. What are the *main thoughts* in this lesson that I have to remember? (The crucial battles that turned the tide of the war.)

4. How many of these *main thoughts* are there? (About five or six.)

5. What do I have to remember about each one of these main thoughts? (The outcome of each battle.)

6. Where in the lesson do I find this information? (*Now he begins to read.*)

JUST LOOK AT THE DIFFERENCE THESE FEW QUESTIONS MAKE.

Now, what exactly has happened here? Your child has invested one or two brief minutes to glance over his lesson from beginning to end. In that short time, he has picked out its main theme and each of its central thoughts. He has built a skeleton of that lesson—an outline of that lesson— a road map of that lesson to follow as he reads.

Now he knows what he is looking for. Now he is walking a lighted path instead of stumbling in the dark. Now, instead of facing a confused jumble of words, he slashes through that lesson with this definite purpose in mind:

What do I have to remember about each one of my main thoughts? (What was the outcome of each battle in this history lesson?)

Now he reads to answer this question. He has *direction*. In one or two minutes, he has a better grasp of that assignment than if he read it aimlessly for a full hour.

HOW HE FINDS THESE MAIN THOUGHTS: SIGN-POSTS IN THE LESSON THAT POINT THEM RIGHT OUT TO HIM.

Fortunately, the authors of your child's books agree with this road-map idea. They too believe that he should first build an outline of the important thoughts in each lesson, and then simply fill in the details.

In order to help him do this, they have built into their books certain signposts that point out these main thoughts. These signposts stick out from the main body of the text. They are the chapter headings, section headings, table of contents, summary paragraphs, and all other vital points set off by capital letters, underlining, italics, and other attention-drawing devices.

They form a book within a book. And by learning how to read them, your child can pick out the main points of that book almost as fast as he can turn its pages.

Let's teach him how to really use them, right now. Let's start with the big signposts, the ones he needs the very first time he picks up a book. The ones that will give him the guts of that entire book in five to ten minutes.

And then let's work our way down to the smaller signposts, the ones that will organize his study each time he's assigned another lesson in that book.

For our first few examples, we'll use this book—the one you're reading now. This will give you a chance to check your own reading habits, to see if you're getting as much information out of each page as you should.

Then we'll go on to examples from standard classbooks. And then we'll see how the same simple techniques apply to everything your child reads—let him pull information out of newspapers, magazines, and so on, almost as fast as he can run his eyes down their pages.

Here we go!

SIGNPOST PARTS OF EVERY BOOK, AND WHAT EACH ONE TELLS YOU

1. THE TITLE.

What it tells you: Actually, a good title should give you, in a single phrase, the main theme of the book. What it is about, and what it is not about. It is your first concrete information about what you are to learn in the pages that follow. Make sure you understand it before you read on.

Example: The title of this book is *How to Double Your Child's Grades in School*. Here is a deliberately long title, containing two separate pieces of information. First, the subject, which is your child's grades in school. Second, a specific goal—to double those grades.

Starting from this title, and knowing exactly what you should get out of this book, you read on with one purpose— *to answer the question "how?"*.

How do I double my child's grades?

To answer this question, you turn to the next big signpost part of the book:

2. THE TABLE OF CONTENTS.

What it tells you: The table of contents takes the grand plan, the ultimate goal you are shooting for, and breaks it down into a step-by-step process. It shows you the steps you have to take, one after another, to attain that goal.

This table of contents is actually a ready-made outline of the book that should be studied carefully before you read one word of its text. By carefully going over this table of contents, you immediately

gain an over-all picture of the skeleton of the book;

see the relationships between each of the various chapters and the main theme of the book;

know exactly where you are going when you start to read—to such a degree that you can even set up a time schedule of so many days per chapter to finish the book when you have to.

For example: In this book, the table of contents is broken down into six main parts, and then into twenty-four chapters.

Let's start with the main parts first, and see how they

give us the over-all plan of the book at a glance. Here they are:

The Simple Strategy of Top Grades. (What we are going to do and how we are going to do it.)

Digging Out the Facts—Reading.

Expressing the Facts—Writing and Reciting.

Mathematics Can Be Fun, If You Do It This Way.

Mastering Facts—The Art of Remembering and Review.

How to Breeze Through Tests.

By simply glancing at these six titles, you immediately see that the book is going to concentrate on reading, writing, and mathematics to the extent of devoting full sections to each of them. Then it's going to show your child how to review for his tests and make top grades in them.

Thus the general goal of doubling your child's grades, which was promised in the title, has now been broken down into specific, step-by-step goals of improving his reading, writing, and arithmetic, helping him over problem areas, and sharpening his ability to take tests.

Now the table of contents goes on to show us more concretely how we're going to accomplish each one of these major goals. It does this by listing the chapter headings under each of them. For example, in the next part of this book, on writing, we find these three chapters:

The First Essentials—Neatness and Penmanship.

Correct Spelling Made Easy.

How to Write As Easily and Quickly As You Think.

Now you can see that there are three steps to improve your child's writing. First, neatness; then spelling; then the actual construction of sentences and paragraphs.

Again we see the grand plan of the book developing before our eyes. From the over-all goal of doubling your child's grades, we have gone on to the six major steps for doing this, and then we have taken one of those steps, which is reading, and learned three ways in which it alone can be improved.

We can do the same thing for each of the other five major parts of the book. Each major part of the book has its own chapter headings underneath it, which show you step by step how you are going to achieve it.

You have now finished reading the title and the table of contents. You have spent perhaps five minutes on the book so far. And yet you now know: 1. What it is going to do for your child, and 2. How it is going to do it, perfectly.

From this point on, you will read simply to answer the questions each one of these chapter headings has raised in your mind. For example, going back to the section on reading again:

How do I improve my child's neatness and penmanship?

How do I get him to spell a word correctly when he has misspelled it everytime before now?

What are the techniques that allow him to write easily and quickly?

At this point you could open to the first page of text, and read faster and with much greater understanding than you have ever read before.

But, before you do this, there are two other big signposts you will want to check, to help you get every ounce of information out of that book.

3.   THE INDEX.

What it tells you: The index is a storehouse of minor topics of special interest to you. There they are alphabetically arranged for instant reference.

For example: Glance at the index of this book. Pick out a topic of special interest to you, or a problem that your child is facing today. For instance, take *fractions*. Look *fractions* up in the index. Turn to the pages indicated there. And *glance at, do not read,* the treatment given to them.

Instantly you can see the concrete, step-by-step methods that make those fractions easy. There's no need to read them, word by word, now, since you'll get up to them later this week. And in the proper time and place in the book, they'll mean far more to you.

But now you know that they're there, and that they're complete. And if you ever have to refer back to them after you finish the book, the index will tell you where they're located at a glance.

And now we turn to the last of our big signposts:

4. THE INTRODUCTION, OR PREFACE, OR FOREWORD.

What it tells you: This is the author's personal message to you, before he gets down to the body of the book. In it, he may

explain why he chose this particular title,

or tell you what compelled him to write the book,

or show you in advance what he is trying to accomplish,

or give you a brief, one or two paragraph condensation of its contents,

or list the main sources from which he got his information,

or list the reasons why this book should be important to you,

or in any other way give you a brief outline of where you will be heading in the book and what benefits it will give you.

It is the personal note, the personal touch that rounds out your quick survey of the book and gives you insight into the author himself and his purpose in writing the book, as well as its contents.

For example: The introduction in this book is divided into three distinct parts, each of which serves a very definite purpose.

Part 1 of the introduction points out the overwhelming importance of top grades to your child's future, and lists ten reasons why they are so vital.

Part 2 shows you that these door-opening top grades are

really not that hard to get and, once he learns the right technique, are actually well within the reach of any student of average or better ability.

Part 3 lists eight specific benefits your child will gain, simply by putting these techniques, which are contained in this book, to work.

The introduction to this book, therefore, is an attempt to encourage you and your child with these three facts: that the goal you bought this book to attain is worth while, that it is obtainable, and that it will give you the results you wish.

When you have finished this introduction, you know exactly what goals you are out to get. Then, reading on through the table of contents, you realize, step by step, exactly how you are going to get them.

In your one brief survey of this book, or any other, you now know exactly what it is you want to get out of it, and where it is located. You are now ready to read the text itself. To cut through it to the heart of its main ideas, and do it almost as fast as your eyes can move down the page.

Let's now turn to the individual chapters, and see how this same exact method—looking for signposts first—can again mine their information for you at a single glance.

In summary:

No matter how bright he may be, your child cannot understand his assignments simply by reading them word by word.

Instead, he must first *pre-read* those assignments—make a quick survey of them *before* he reads to uncover their main thoughts.

He does this, not only with each chapter he is assigned, but with each new book that he studies.

He finds the main ideas of each of these books by checking the following four signpost parts of every book:

1. The title.
2. The table of contents.
3. The index.
4. The introduction or preface.

When he lifts these signpost parts out of the text and arranges them in order, your child will have at his fingertips an outline of the main thoughts of that entire book.

He can then read each individual chapter in order, with perfect understanding of how it ties into the chapter that has gone before it, the chapter that follows it, and the main theme of the book as a whole.

Now let's see how easy it is to pull out the main thoughts of each chapter in the same exact way.

CHAPTER 7

SIGNPOST PARTS OF EVERY CHAPTER, AND
WHAT EACH ONE TELLS YOU

In the section above, when we looked at the four big signposts in every book—the title, the table of contents, the index, and the introduction—we used this book as our example. And we used *you* as our subject, to show you how these big signposts can help even an intelligent adult get far more information out of any book, in far less time.

The same technique is used by your child the first time he opens a new textbook. Using this technique, he gets a bird's-eye view of the entire course, the first day he begins it. During the rest of the school term, chapter by chapter, he is merely filling in important details, deepening his understanding of the grand plan he discovered in his first survey of the book.

To do this, he applies to each individual chapter the same quick-survey technique he used at the beginning of the book.

To illustrate this technique in action, let's turn now to three fresh examples. To typical textbooks he will meet in school.

And let us see exactly what he should do to them, step by step. How much material he has left—and how much he has discarded—when he has finished reducing them to their main thoughts. And how he burns that material into his memory, for good.

Here are these examples, first reproduced word for word (I suggest you simply glance over them briefly now):

CHAPTER FROM A SIXTH-GRADE TEXTBOOK ON ENGLISH.

THE FOUR KINDS OF SENTENCES.

A declarative sentence makes a statement. It is followed by a period.

EXAMPLE: Poochie is a dog.

An interrogative sentence asks something. It is a question. It is followed by a question mark.

EXAMPLE: Do you have a dog?

To find the subject of an interrogative sentence, simply turn it into a declarative sentence.

EXAMPLE: You do have a dog.

An exclamatory sentence shows surprise or excitement. It is followed by an exclamation point.

EXAMPLE: What a thrilling thought!

Sometimes an exclamatory sentence has to be changed to a simple declarative sentence before it is clear what the subject and predicate are.

EXAMPLE:

A. Exclamatory:

How Dick and John hate each other!

B. The same sentence turned into a declarative sentence:

Dick and John hate each other, how.

An imperative sentence gives a command. It is followed by either a period or an exclamation point.

EXAMPLE: Tell me where you were!

In an imperative sentence the word *you* is always understood to be the subject.

EXAMPLE: (You) tell me where you were!

FIRST SECTION FROM A CHAPTER IN A HIGH
SCHOOL TEXTBOOK ON WORLD HISTORY: (*I have
numbered each paragraph at the end.*)

THE GREEKS

I. The Background

The ancient Greeks developed the first government
that might be called democratic and the first great civili-
zation to take permanent root on the mainland of
Europe. Yet the Greek civilization that matured almost
twenty-five hundred years ago was by no means purely
European in character. The Greeks inhabited the west-
ern coast of Asia Minor and the islands dotting the
Aegean Sea as well as the European peninsula we call
Greece. They also inherited some of the legacy of the
older Near Eastern civilizations, probably passed on to
them through the Aegean civilization. (1)

Aegean Civilization

Aegean Civilization, which lasted for some two
thousand years down to about 1100 B.C., apparently
centered on the island of Crete at the southern entrance
to the Aegean Sea. Crete had many natural advantages.
Its mild climate favored agriculture; the sea gave it
some protection against invasion and conquest and at
the same time promoted seafaring. Located at the cross-
roads of the eastern Mediterranean, Crete was close
enough to Asia, Africa and Europe for daring seamen
to sail their primitive vessels to Egypt and Greece. Its
geographical position doubtless made trade and piracy
the natural occupations of the islanders. (2)

When copper and the manufacture of bronze were
introduced, probably from Phoenicia or elsewhere in
Asia Minor at some time before 3000 B.C., civilization
began on Crete. The civilization is termed Minoan, from
Minos, a legendary king, and archeologists have divided
it into three main chronological periods (3):

Early Minoan—down to 2300 B.C.
Middle Minoan—2300 to 1600 B.C.
Late Minoan— 1600 to 1100 B.C. (4)

Each of these three main periods is subdivided into three segments, from I to III. The greatest flowering of culture on Crete seems to have occurred during the Middle Minoan III and the late Minoan I and II, between 1700 and 1400 B.C. (5)

We must say "seems to have occurred," for our knowledge of ancient Crete is still incomplete. Up to the beginning of the twentieth century it was so sketchy that no methodical approach to its civilization was possible. Then, in 1900, the British archeologist, Sir Arthur Evans, acting on a well-founded hunch, began excavations at Cnossus in central Crete, a few miles inland from the north shore of the island. He struck "pay-dirt" almost at once and started to uncover what was evidently a very large and very ancient palace, which he termed the "palace of Minos." Subsequent diggings by Evans and others disclosed the sites of more than a hundred towns that had existed before 1500 B.C., a goodly amount of pottery, and stretches of paved road. (6)

More recently, hundreds of tablets with Aegean writing have also come to light, both in Crete itself and on the Greek mainland. Although no Minoan equivalent of the Rosetta stone has been found, one scholar announced in 1953 that by using the techniques of cryptography, he had begun the work of deciphering the tablets. This discovery may eventually revolutionize our knowledge of Crete. Meanwhile, we have very little sure information on Minoan politics, though it is conjectured that Crete, like Egypt, had despotic priest-kings who ruled with the aid of a central bureaucracy. (7)

The archeological remains, however, provide convincing evidence that the Minoans were great builders, engineers and artists. The palace at Cnossus was at least two stories high and filled an area equivalent to a city block. A city in miniature, it had running water, a sewage system, and a kind of playground used for dancing, wrestling and other sports. The palace was begun in the Middle Minoan I period and was often repaired and altered, particularly after Middle Minoan II after a destructive earthquake. As a result, the excavated palace is a maze of storerooms, courtyards, corridors, workshops, living quarters, and government offices. Sir Arthur Evans realized that he had very likely discovered

the actual building that had inspired the Greek legend of
the labyrinth to which the early Greeks were forced to
send sacrificial victims. (8)

The skilled craftsmen of Crete apparently copied
Egyptian techniques. They did marvelous work, from
huge jars, as high as a man, to delicate little cups, no
thicker than an eggshell, decorated with birds, flowers,
fishes and other natural designs. Painters executed large
frescos of kings and warriors on the palace walls. Ivory,
gold and jewels were used for the inlaid gaming boards
of the kings and for exquisite statuettes, less than a foot
high, of the bare-breasted snake-goddess who was ap-
parently one of the chief objects of worship. (9)

Crete at the height of its power may have controlled
an empire including the other Aegean islands and,
perhaps, the Aegean shores of Asia Minor and Greece.
The recent work on Aegean tablets, however, suggests
that Crete itself may have become an outpost of the
Greek mainland rather early. The extent of Minoan
political influence is highly uncertain; there is less doubt
about Minoan *cultural* influence, which very likely
reached to other parts of the Aegean world. (10)

A nineteenth-century German, Heinrich Schliemann,
undertook excavations at Troy, in northwest Asia Minor,
the scene of Homer's *Iliad,* and at Mycenae on the Greek
mainland, the home of Agamemnon, the leader of the
Greek forces in the Trojan War of Homer's epic. Schlie-
mann loved Homer so deeply that he devoted his life
to proving that the Homeric Trojan War was not poetic
invention but historical fact. Schliemann's determina-
tion resulted in a great archeological romance—early
poverty, business success in America, mastery of the
Greek language, marriage to a Greek lady (she could
recite Homer from memory!), and finally, later in life,
discovery of the site of Troy, though it turned out that
what he uncovered was a later city built on the ruins of
Homeric Troy. (11)

Thanks to Schliemann and later experts, we now
know that by 1400 B.C. Troy and a group of cities
centered at Mycenae in Greece had attained a degree of
civilization strikingly similar to what had apparently
been reached in Crete centuries earlier. Mycenaean pot-

tery, though made of different materials, is similar to Minoan in design and ornamentation. At Mycenae, the kings were buried in large underground tombs, shaped like beehives, which resembled tombs built earlier in Crete. The cities on the mainland, however, built much more elaborate fortifications than did those of Crete. (12)

By about 1600 B.C., sporadic groups of invaders were filtering down from the north. They appear to have been Greeks, a people who spoke a language probably much like the classic Greek. The first Greeks seemed to have mixed rather peaceably with the existing populations of Greece, the Aegean islands, and Asia Minor, and to have acquired the Aegean culture that flourished at Mycenae and elsewhere. Later Greek invaders were more warlike and destructive. As tribe after tribe pushed south, the old Aegean civilization grew steadily weaker until it finally perished about 1100 B.C. By that time, the Greeks controlled the entire Aegean area, including Crete itself. (13)

The Setting of Greek Civilization

The forces of nature played a large part in shaping Greek civilization. The climate and geography of the Greek homeland have changed little since ancient times. As in the Mediterranean area as a whole, the rains come mainly between September and May. The summers are long, sunny and dry, but because of the sea breezes they are not intolerably hot. People can live outdoors during the greater part of the year, and they can grow olives and other semi-tropical fruit. The sharply indented coastline and the profusion of mountains make a magnificent natural setting. Nature combines such lavish amounts of sunshine and scenery only in California and a few other parts of the world. (14)

Greece, however, has never had the immense fertile acres typical of California. The quality of the soil is poor, and the valleys and plains, squeezed by the mountains, are on a miniature scale. The rivers and streams are too swift and shallow for navigation; they flood in the rainy season, then dwindle to a trickle or dry up altogether.

Local springs can supply the minimum needs of the population during the dry season, but they are not adequate for extensive irrigation. (15)

Greece, in short, has never afforded men an easy living, though it has often provided a reasonably pleasant one. The farms and orchards of ancient Greece produced barley and other grains, fruit, wine, honey and little else. Meat was a rarity. (16)

The Greek homeland, however, had one great geographical advantage: its situation encouraged navigation, even by the rather timid. The irregular coasts of the mainland and the islands provided sheltered anchorages; destructive storms seldom occurred during the long summer, the great season of navigation; and the vessels could go for hundreds of miles without ever losing sight of land. Travel in ships propelled by sails or oars or a combination of the two was cheaper, swifter and more comfortable than an up-hill and down-dale journey overland. The Greeks, consequently, built up an active maritime trade. (17)

The geography of Greece favored political decentralization. In the valleys of the Tigris, the Euphrates and the Nile, the absence of natural barriers to travel had helped the building of large empires. In Greece, on the other hand, the frequent mountains and countless bays and gulfs impeded land communication. The individual valleys and plains, both on the mainland and on the islands, were natural geographic and economic units; they served as separate political units, too. (18)

The political unit was the *polis* or city-state, which included a city and the surrounding countryside. Most of the city-states were exceedingly limited in area; Greece, although a small country, contained many dozens of them. By modern standards, the average Greek city was at best a mere town, and many of its inhabitants were primarily farmers. A strong point, which could be readily defended against attack, was the nucleus of the city. A familiar example is the Acropolis at Athens, with its commanding height and its steep and difficult approaches. (19)

FROM A COLLEGE TEXTBOOK ON BUSINESS ADMINISTRATION. (*I have numbered each paragraph at the end.*)

CHAPTER 2: FIVE ROADS TO COST REDUCTION

Every management is faced with a continuing need to effect cost reduction. Somehow or other we think of these reductions as available principally in the manufacturing process, but this is not the sole area for expense reduction. There are at least five channels through which important savings can be effected. These are (1):

1. Raw materials.
2. The costs of capital equipment.
3. Manufacturing costs.
4. Sales expense.
5. General and administrative overhead expense (including the office). (2)

Although there are some procedures in common

which you can use in endeavoring to reduce expenses along these five avenues, for the most part the approaches must be different. (3)

Road 1: Raw Materials

Raw materials costs vary greatly with industries. Most companies have long since worked out the average percentage of the sales dollar paid for raw materials and supplies. If you can make a comparison of this percentage for your company against other companies in your industry, you may have an excellent starting point. And even where you can't do this, or the comparison is favorable to your company, it nevertheless may pay you to study the ways of lowering the cost of raw materials. Here are the principal devices which companies have used (4):

1. Development of carefully prepared purchasing specifications, which demand raw material which is good enough for your manufacturing process but not of such high quality that your costs go up without a compensating increase in the price of your ultimate product. (5)

2. Inspection of incoming materials to make certain that they meet these specifications. (6)

3. Tracing back difficulties in the manufacturing process to raw material imperfections. (7)

4. Modifications of manufacturing processes to eliminate the necessity for certain raw materials and supplies. (8)

5. Substitution of other kinds of raw materials. (9)

6. Control over the sources of raw materials either by purchase of supply sources (vertical integration) or by long term contractual arrangements. (10)

Road 2: The Costs of Capital Equipment

Piled upon manufacturing costs and material costs must be cost of capital equipment used. Typical of such costs would be depreciation, replacement, maintenance and interest on borrowed capital. (11)

A great many companies tie up a lot of money in semi-finished or finished inventories. It's useful to make an occasional check as to the amount so tied up and compare it with previous checks. (12)

Because of inventory pricing policies used by accountants at the close of the year, many a company goes through the year thinking that it has had a profitable operation, only to discover that the inventory pricing has sharply reduced the expected profit. (13)

In Chapter 4 we shall consider capital financing in more detail, so we shall not make further comment here. (14)

Road 3: Manufacturing Costs

Manufacturing costs normally consist of labor plus material plus manufacturing overhead. (15)

Labor opens up a large area for study. It includes proper original selection, adequate training of workers, incentives, supervision, standards and control. It may involve aptitude testing, skill training, time and motion study, work simplification, etc. (16)

Reduction of manufacturing overhead may involve studies of supervision, maintenance and other indirect labor; of inspection and quality control; of fuel, light and power; of fire, safety and insurance protection; of idle equipment charges; of proper utilization of the space available; etc. (17)

Design of new equipment for production involves consideration of manufacturing methods and the capital investment required. (18)

Proper lighting has been responsible for worthwhile increases in productivity and reduction of accidents. Improvements have also resulted from painting of walls and machines, reduction of noise, better ventilation, etc. (19)

Materials handling is usually another fertile field for investigation. The movement and storage of raw materials, work in progress and finished goods can add considerably to the final cost of manufactured goods. (20)

Studies of productive operations may readily include operations research, whereby mathematics is applied to determine the optimum or best manufacturing conditions. Typical would be job lot size to derive the greatest advantage from manufacturing operations;

proper inventories of raw materials, partial assemblies, semi-finished products and finished products. (21)

Road 4: Sales Expense

Over the present century there has been a reversal of the relationship of manufacturing cost to marketing costs. At one time manufacturing costs represented more than half the sales price of an article, but these costs have relatively receded so that today, in most companies, the sales costs represent more than half the sales price. Contributing to this increase in sales cost have been such items as warehousing, transportation, advertising, packaging, direct sales costs, and the constant price attrition of competition. Sales overhead, too, has increased through the addition of market research, sales promotion specialists, automatic vending equipment, more sales supervision, etc. (22)

Many sales managers have virtually become sales controllers. Their functions increasingly are those of analysis and control. They need both the accountant's figures as to sales expense and the statistician's figures as to sales analysis. The latter will normally show dollar and quantity sales by salesman, by territory, by customer and product. Wherever the sales manager detects a falling off in some one of these areas, he applies effort to change the condition. (23)

Road 5: General and Administrative Expense

The fifth avenue of cost reduction consists of analysis of general and administrative expenses. In the normal company these cover such items as salaries of executives and office employees, office expense, interest, property depreciation, taxes, insurance, donations, legal fees, consultants, investigation of possible mergers, economic services and other general business expenses. (24)

Savings through determined effort here can be large indeed. (25)

In Summary

The five roads to cost reduction are:
1. Raw materials.
2. The costs of capital equipment.

3. Manufacturing costs.
4. Sales expense.
5. General and administrative expense. (26)

Once possible economies have been uncovered it is necessary to prosecute them vigorously, lest they fail of accomplishment through inertia and resistance to change. (27)

NOW LET'S GET TO WORK ON THOSE CHAPTERS. HERE'S HOW THE CHAPTER SIGNPOSTS BREAK THEM DOWN FOR YOUR CHILD, IN MINUTES.

As you could tell at a glance, it's simply not enough for your child to just read these sample chapters, word by word, from start to finish. If he tries to do this, he will confuse detail with main idea, and he will remember almost nothing when he is through reading.

What your child needs is a key—a system—that will unlock that mass of words and pull out the main ideas for him.

This key is PRE-READING. The ability to read chapter signposts at a glance, and use them to pinpoint the main ideas of the chapter, one after the other, and give purpose and direction to his reading.

There are eight signpost parts of every chapter that your child should know as well as his own name. Let's review them one by one, and see how they pull the main ideas right out of these chapters *before* your child begins to read the text.

1. THE CHAPTER TITLE

What it tells you: What the chapter is about. What it includes and does not include.

Examples: In the first chapter, the title *The Four Kinds of Sentences* shows your child that there are a specific number of definitions to learn—four. And each of these definitions describes a different kind of sentence. Thus he knows immediately what he is looking for—definitions—and how many he must find—four.

The third sample chapter gives the same information in its title. *Five Roads to Cost Reduction* tells your child that he must find a specific number of ways to reduce costs—five—and must discover how and in what ways each one works.

The title of the second chapter *THE GREEKS, I. The Background* is more vague. It does not tell how many parts are to follow. But it does tell your child that he is going to study the Greeks, and what he is going to look for in the first section of the chapter is the effect of their background upon them. He must now read on, to the next chapter signposts, to discover what he must find out about their background. To do this, he turns to:

2.   THE SECTION HEADINGS

What they tell him: The section headings break down the over-all chapter heading into its main parts. They list the names and number of important subjects to be covered in the chapter. Reading them quickly, without the intervening text, gives him the skeleton of the chapter.

Examples: The section headings in our third sample chapter read as follows:

Road 1: *Raw Materials*
Road 2: *The Costs of Capital Equipment*
Road 3: *Manufacturing Costs*
Road 4: *Sales Expense*
Road 5: *General and Administrative Expense*

Here are the five roads to cost reduction mentioned in the chapter title, laid out for him at a glance. He now knows the entire structure of the chapter. His only task now is to read the text, and find out *how* he can reduce costs in each of these areas.

In sample chapter two, however, the section headings are fewer in number and more vague. They are:

Aegean Civilization, and

The Setting of Greek Civilization

These give him the two main sources of the background of Greek civilization. But they do not yet give him enough information on what he is to find out about each. Therefore he must go on to further signposts, which we will describe in a moment.

And in our first sample chapter, there are no section headings at all. So he checks the next chapter signpost, which is:

3. PARAGRAPH HEADS OR BOLD PRINTS

What they tell him: The main topic of each paragraph. What the paragraph contains, boiled down into a single phrase.

For example: In this first sample chapter, the author has carefully stated the name of each kind of sentence. Listing them in order, we have:

Declarative sentence

Interrogative sentence

Exclamatory sentence

Imperative sentence

Immediately, your child knows the names of the four kinds of sentences he is to learn in this lesson. Now all he has to do is read the text, and find out a definition for each of them.

In the other two sample chapters, there are no paragraph headings. And so we turn to the next chapter signpost:

4. INTRODUCTORY PARAGRAPHS

What they tell him: Here the author points out to the student what to look for in the text that follows. He gives an introduction to the chapter, ties it into the chapters that came before it, and reveals the main thought or thoughts in the material in the remainder of the chapter.

For example: In the second sample chapter, the authors begin with this introductory paragraph (for the purposes of this survey, let's break the paragraph apart, point out each of its main thoughts, and state the purpose):

"The ancient Greeks developed the first government that might be called democratic and the first great civilization to take permanent root on the mainland of Europe."

(This is the introduction to the chapter, pointing out the importance of the Greeks to us all.)

"Yet the Greek civilization that matured almost twenty-five hundred years ago was by no means purely European in character."

(Now the authors lead us from the introductory sentence to the non-European background of the Greeks. This is what they are going to discuss in the material that follows.)

"The Greeks inhabited the western coast of Asia Minor and the islands dotting the Aegean Sea as well as the European peninsula we call Greece."

(We are told the first important influence, the geographical setting.)

"They also inherited some of the legacy of the older Near Eastern civilizations, probably passed on to them through the Aegean Civilization."

(And now we are told the second vital influence, the Aegean civilization.)

Thus the introductory paragraph confirms the two main divisions in the chapter—the Aegean Civilization and the Geographical Setting—that were revealed earlier by a survey of the section headings. Now your child knows he's on the right track. But he is still looking for further subdivisions. So he continues the search to the next chapter signpost.

Usually he would next check:

5. THE SUMMARY OR CLOSING PARAGRAPHS

What they tell him: The summary paragraphs are the author's last words on the chapter. They are his own outline of the material he has covered in this chapter before he passes on to the next. They are a declaration of what *he* deems important out of all the material your child has just read.

Sometimes he sums this material up in one paragraph. Sometimes he outlines each idea in a separate phrase, paragraphs it, and may even number it. Sometimes he rephrases the important points in the form of questions.

In any case, these final words deserve careful study *before* your child begins the text.

For example: Since there is no summary paragraph in our second sample chapter, let's use the one in the third chapter as our example. It reads:

"In Summary:

The five roads to cost reduction are:

1. *Raw Materials.*
2. *The Costs of Capital Equipment.*
3. *Manufacturing Costs.*
4. *Sales Expense.*
5. *General and Administrative Expense.*

Once possible economies have been uncovered, it is necessary to prosecute them vigorously, lest they fail of accomplishment through inertia and resistance to change."

These sentences confirm what your child has already discovered. He is now doubly sure that he has the five roads to cost reduction firmly outlined in his mind; and, especially on the basis of the last paragraph in the summary, now only has to read on to discover how he can reduce costs in each of these areas.

He now turns to the next chapter signpost:

6. THE FIRST SENTENCE OF EACH PARAGRAPH

What they tell him: As you remember, this Pre-Reading, this quick survey of an entire chapter before your child begins the text, is essentially a search. A search for the main thoughts of that chapter—for a quick outline of that chapter that tells him exactly what he is looking for and where to find it.

This search begins with the chapter title, and continues, one by one, with each of the following chapter signposts till your child has uncovered those main ideas—till he has built his outline.

At this point, when your child has located the main ideas in the chapter, he stops the Pre-Reading and begins the text. The Pre-Reading is a search for the chapter's main ideas. When he has found them, he begins to read.

Therefore he does not check all the chapter signposts in each Pre-Reading of each chapter. He checks only enough signposts to give him his main ideas, and then ignores the others.

For example, in the third sample chapter, he needed only to read the chapter title, and then the section heads, to find out what the main ideas were—the five roads to cost reduction. Therefore he would not even glance at the other chapter signposts, but begin reading the text immediately to find out how he could reduce costs in each of these areas.

In the same way, in sample chapter one, he needed only to read the chapter title, then check to see that there were no section headings, and then simply pick up his main ideas out of the underlined paragraph headings. At that point, he had the four kinds of sentences, and would immediately begin to read the text to find a definition for each.

However, it is the second sample chapter that forces him to make a deeper survey. In this second chapter, he has read the title, found only two section headings, found no paragraph heads, discovered that the introductory paragraph merely confirms the two main ideas he learned from the sections headings, and again found that there was no summary paragraph.

So what he has gained from his first five signposts is this. He knows that he is to learn about the background of Greek civilization. And he knows that there are two sources of this background—the Aegean civilization, and the geographical setting of Greece.

What he still does *not* know, however, is *what each of these sources contributed* to Greek civilization. He has to uncover these contributions—how many there were and what each of them was—before he can begin reading with definite, clear-cut goals in mind.

Therefore he probes deeper. He turns to the next chapter signpost—the first sentence of each paragraph.

In most cases, especially if the author has done his work well, these first sentences are called *topic sentences*. They give the main idea of the paragraph, and let the remaining sentences fill in the details.

So, if your child takes the first sentence of each paragraph and strings them together, he should have a fairly good outline of the main ideas in the chapter.

Unfortunately, this method is not as automatic or as clear cut as those using the first five signposts. Your child has to use more judgment in weeding out paragraphs that don't really contain main ideas.

But in those rare cases when the first five signposts don't do the job, he must go on with the sixth. Let's see how this method opens up the main ideas in this massive second chapter:

For example: The first sentences of each paragraph in the second chapter are these (We will give each sentence the number of the paragraph it comes from. And we will leave out the first, introductory sentence, since we have already covered it):

"*AEGEAN CIVILIZATION*

2.　*Aegean civilization, which lasted for some two thou-*

sand years down to about 1100 B.C., apparently centered on the island of Crete at the southern entrance to the Aegean Sea.

3. When copper and the manufacture of bronze were introduced, probably from Phoenicia or elsewhere in Asia Minor at some time before 3000 B.C., civilization began on Crete.

4. (Unimportant)
5. (Unimportant)
6. (Unimportant)
7. (Unimportant)

8. The archeological remains, however, provide convincing evidence that the Minoans were great builders, engineers and artists.

9. (Unimportant)

10. Crete at the height of its power may have controlled an empire including the other Aegean islands and, perhaps, the Aegean shores of Asia Minor and Greece.

11. (Unimportant)

12. Thanks to Schliemann and later experts, we now know that by 1400 B.C. Troy and a group of cities centered at Mycenae in Greece had attained a degree of civilization strikingly similar to what had apparently been reached in Crete centuries earlier.

13. (Unimportant)

THE SETTING OF GREEK CIVILIZATION

14. The forces of nature played a large part in shaping Greek civilization.

15. (Unimportant)
16. (Unimportant)

17. The Greek homeland, however, had one great geographical advantage: its situation encouraged navigation, even by the very timid.

18. The geography of Greece favored political decentralization.

19. (Unimportant)"

These are the first sentences of each important paragraph in the chapter. Already, in choosing them, the boiling-down process has begun. Already unnecessary words and details have been thrown out. Your child is looking only for main ideas. He therefore chooses only those paragraphs that contain those main ideas.

But how does he know which paragraphs to choose and which to leave out? In a very simple way.

He already knows the main theme of the chapter, *THE GREEKS, I. The Background,* which was given to him in the chapter title.

He already knows the two main sources of that background, *Aegean Civilization and the Geographical Setting,* which were given to him in the section headings.

He does not know, however, how many divisions each of these two sources have, and what each contributed to Greek civilization. This is the information he is looking for in the first sentence of each paragraph.

And he is looking only for big contributions, not details.

Therefore he will judge each sentence by these two simple rules:

1. *They must talk about the main theme of the chapter, and not about some side issue.*

In this case, they must talk about the Aegean contribution to the background of Greek civilization, or about the geographical contribution to that background, and about nothing else.

2. *They must bring in a new main point, and not merely furnish details about a main point brought up by the paragraph before.*

These are the two rules of what to leave in and what to throw out. They are quite simple to follow. Let's see how they eliminate most of the paragraphs in this second sample chapter, and leave only the main points.

Sentence 2: Mentions Crete as the center of Aegean civilization. Leave it in.

Sentence 3:   Shows high civilization, based on metals, that Crete contributed to Greeks. Leave it in.

Sentence 4:   Just dates of Minoan culture. No contribution to Greeks. Throw it out.

Sentence 5:   More Minoan periods. Out.

Sentence 6:   Says nothing but that our knowledge of Crete is incomplete. No contribution here. Probably a side issue. Throw it out.

Sentence 7:   Another scientific side issue. Out.

Sentence 8:   Now we get to basic contributions from the Minoans—building, engineering, artistry. Leave it in.

Sentence 9:   Details about Minoan art. We already have art in the sentence above. Leave it out.

Sentence 10:   Discusses Minoan seafaring, politics, war —all picked up by Greeks later on. Leave it in.

Sentence 11:   Side issue. Interesting but not important. Throw it out.

Sentence 12:   Identifies other centers of Aegean civilization. Now we know there were two—Crete and Mycenae. And we know that they both made essentially the same contributions. A good find. Leave it in.

Sentence 13:   Talks about invaders, not Aegeans. Not on topic we want. Throw it out.

Sentence 14:   Identifies forces of nature as first great geographical influence of Greeks. Leave it in.

Sentence 15:   Detail under natural forces (soil conditions). Leave it out.

Sentence 16:   Mere comment on effect of natural forces. Covered already by sentence 14 above. Out.

Sentence 17:   New effect of geographical setting— navigable water. Important. Leave it in.

Sentence 18:   A third main effect—political decentralization. Leave it in.

Sentence 19:   A detail about the political centralization mentioned in the paragraph above—the name of the city-state. Not a main point. Throw it out.

Now what has your child left, after he's thrown out the unimportant paragraphs? Let's see.

Taking the title and section headings as they are, and further boiling down the first sentences to a phrase or two each, this is what he should end up with:

THE GREEKS, I. BACKGROUND

Aegean Civilization.

Located at Crete, Troy and Mycenae. All made the same contributions.

Contributions were in metals, building, engineering, art, politics, seafaring, warfare.

The Setting of Greek Civilization.

Greek civilization was shaped by (1) the forces of nature; (2) by the easily navigable waters surrounding Greece; and (3) by the Greek terrain, which made for political decentralization.

With this outline at his fingertips, your child now begins reading the text to make sure he understands each of these main points thoroughly.

However, had he not been able to get all the main points from the first six chapter signposts, he still had two more that might have been able to help him. Let's briefly glance at these now:

7. ILLUSTRATIONS

What they tell him: Illustrations, charts, graphs, photographs, etc., are pictorial presentations of the main ideas in each chapter. They boil down great amounts of information, and give them to your child at a single glance. Often they convey information that simply could never be put into words.

For example: The map in sample chapter two shows the geographical setting of Greece quite vividly. At a glance, your child sees the wonderful advantages Greek mariners had to explore the entire Mediterranean. This confirms the main idea shown in the outline above concerning the easily navigable waters surrounding Greece.

And as our last chapter signpost:

8. MARGINAL TITLES

What they tell him: Marginal titles take the main point of each paragraph, and set it in bold type in the margin next to the text of the paragraph. They thus build a walking outline of the chapter for you in the margin. Unfortunately, however, they are not used in modern textbooks to any great extent; and your child must get the same information from the paragraph headings mentioned above.

For example: None of our three sample chapters uses marginal titles. However, if our second sample chapter did use them, it would look like this:

BEGINNINGS OF MINOAN CIVILIZATION

3.   *"When copper and the manufacture of bronze were introduced, probably from Phoenecia or elsewhere in Asia Minor at some time before 3000 B.C., civilization began on Crete. The civilization is termed Minoan, from Minos, a legendary king, and archeologists have divided it into three main chronological periods. . ."*

In summary:

When he is reading an individual chapter or lesson in a book, your child uses the same Pre-Reading, quick-survey technique that he first used to understand the book as a whole.

He uses this quick-survey technique to pull out the main ideas from the chapter before he begins to read it.

He finds these main ideas by checking the following eight chapter signposts:

1. The Chapter Title.
2. The Section Headings.
3. The Paragraph Headings or Bold Prints.
4. The Introductory Paragraphs.
5. The Summary Paragraphs.
6. The First Sentence of Each Paragraph.
7. The Illustrations.
8. The Marginal Titles.

When he lifts these chapter signposts out of the text and arranges them in order, your child will have an outline of the main thoughts of that chapter at his fingertips.

He may then flash-read that chapter—merely skimming over the unimportant details—and concentrating only on definite information on each of these main thoughts.

We now turn to a simple trick that will automatically show your child exactly what information he must look for on each one of those main points.

CHAPTER 8

Now let's list the outlines your child has built by Pre-Reading the three sample chapters in this book.

In the first sample chapter—the simplest one—here is his outline:

THE FOUR KINDS OF SENTENCES.
1. Declarative sentence.
2. Interrogative sentence.
3. Exclamatory sentence.
4. Imperative sentence.

In the second sample chapter, this is the outline he's worked out:

THE GREEKS, I. BACKGROUND
Aegean Civilization.

Located at Crete, Troy and Mycenae. All made the same contributions.

Contributions were in metals, building, engineering, politics, seafaring, warfare.

The Setting of Greek Civilization.

Greek civilization was shaped by:
1. The forces of nature.
2. The easily navigable waters surrounding Greece.
3. The Greek terrain, which made for political decentralization.

And in the third sample chapter, the outline emerged like this:

FIVE ROADS TO COST REDUCTION.
1. Raw Materials.
2. Capital Equipment.
3. Manufacturing Costs.
4. Sales Expense.
5. General and Administrative Expense.

At this point, your child has the main ideas of each sample chapter at his fingertips. But his knowledge of the chapter is, of course, still incomplete. Now he must read the text itself, *to find out what he should know about each one of these main points.*

And how does he tell—again in advance of actually reading the text—exactly what it is that he should know about each one of these points?

The answer is simplicity itself. He merely

1. *Turns each one of these main points into a question.* And then

2. *Reads the text to find out their answers.*

It's as easy as that. Now let's see this question-and-answer technique in action.

THE SIX BASIC QUESTIONS.

Any idea—any word, any phrase, any sentence—can be turned into a question simply by putting in front of it one of these six little words:

What?
Why?
Where?
When?
Who?
How?

These are extremely valuable words. You should make your child memorize them from the very first grade on. They have been called, and rightly so, the Six Tiny Keys to Knowledge. Let's see what they can do when we apply them to the main thoughts in each one of our sample chapters.

TURNING THE FIRST SAMPLE OUT-LINE INTO A SERIES OF QUESTIONS

First, your child starts with the chapter title. Placing the word *what* in front of it, he gets:

What are the four kinds of sentences?

This question has already been answered for him by the section headings in his outline—declarative, interrogative, exclamatory, and imperative. So he puts the same question to each of these four kinds of sentences, like this:

What is the definition of a declarative sentence?
What is the definition of an interrogative sentence?
What is the definition of an exclamatory sentence?
What is the definition of an imperative sentence?

Your child now knows exactly what information he is looking for about each one of his main points. He now reads to answer these questions, to discover that information, and skims over everything else.

TURNING THE SECOND SAMPLE OUT-LINE INTO A SERIES OF QUESTIONS

Again, your child first starts with the chapter title. Placing the word *what* in front of it, he gets:

What are the background sources of Greek civilization?

This question has already been answered for him in the two section headings—the Aegean civilization and the geographical setting. So he questions each one of the section headings in turn, like this:

Placing the word *where* in front of the first section heading, he gets:

Where was Aegean civilization located?

His paragraph headings answer this question—at Crete, Troy and Mycenae. So he asks again:

What were their contributions to Greek civilization?

Again he has the answers—in metals, building, engineering, politics, seafaring, warfare. So he asks again:

What did the Aegean civilization contribute to the Greek Civilization in metals?

What did it contribute in building?

What did it contribute in engineering?

What did it contribute in politics?

What did it contribute in seafaring?

What did it contribute in warfare?

These are the questions in this section that your child reads on to answer. He then turns to the second section, and questions its heading.

What were the geographical factors that helped shape Greek civilization?

He has his answers—forces of nature, navigable waters, rough terrain. So he questions each one of these factors in turn.

How did the forces of nature help shape Greek civilization?

How did navigable waters help shape Greek civilization?

How did the rough terrain help shape Greek civilization?

Your child now knows exactly what information he is looking for about each one of his main points. He now reads to answer these questions, to discover that information, and skims over everything else.

TURNING THE THIRD SAMPLE CHAPTER INTO A SERIES OF QUESTIONS

Once again, your child first starts with the chapter title. Placing the word *what* in front of it, he gets:

What are the five roads to cost reduction?

His section headings give him the answers—raw materials, capital equipment, manufacturing costs, sales expense, and general and administrative expenses. So he questions each one of these section headings in turn, like this:

How can my firm cut raw materials costs?

How can my firm cut capital equipment costs?

How can my firm cut manufacturing costs?

How can my firm cut sales costs?

How can my firm cut general and administrative costs?

Your child now knows exactly what information he is looking for about each one of his main points. He now reads to answer these questions, to discover this information, and skims over everything else.

HOW YOUR CHILD CAN USE THIS QUESTION-AND-ANSWER TECHNIQUE TO FLASH THROUGH CURRENT-EVENTS READING, IN NEWSPAPERS AND MAGAZINES

Your child has now finished his Pre-Reading of each chapter. He has done this Pre-Reading in three simple and logical steps:

1. He has checked the chapter signposts.

2. He has used them to pull out the main ideas of the chapter.

3. He has turned those main ideas into questions, and will now read to answer them.

This Pre-Reading, quick survey, question-and-answer technique is one of the most powerful tools of thought your child will ever learn. You should demand that he practice it over and over again, till he becomes an expert at it.

He should use it, not only for his textbooks, but for every piece of written material he reads. It will literally cut his reading time in half, and double the amount of information he remembers from the article.

For example, let's apply this same technique to a few

newspaper and magazine headlines, to see how it pinpoints the important information in them for him at a glance.

First, let's look at newspaper headlines, with the headlines first, and then our questions immediately afterward.

SCHOOL BOARD AGAIN TARGET OF PICKETS
Why?

CORE SPOKESMAN PRESSES DEMAND FOR PUPIL'S TRANSFER.
What pupil?
Why has the transfer been refused?
What exactly does the CORE spokesman want done?
What are the chances of its being done?
What will happen if it is done? If it is not done?

CUBA BANK ASSETS BLOCKED BY U.S.
What assets?
How much are they?
Why are they being blocked?
What will happen because of this block? By Cuba? By Russia? By the United States?

KENNEDY, WIRTZ CONFER ON MOVE IN RAIL CRISIS
What is the crisis?
How long will it last?
What will be its effects?
What will the government do to meet it?
How soon can they act?
What will happen if they are successful? If they are not?
What will happen next?

You can see immediately what this technique does. It centers your child's attention on the important issues, and prevents him from being distracted by minor details. It forces him to define those main issues, trace their causes and effects, judge how long they'll last, and estimate what will happen next. It pulls the guts out of the article for him, as fast as he can run his eye down the page.

And this same technique works equally well in magazines, as in this example:

A PLAN TO FREE CUBA
What is it?
Who is its author?
How qualified is he?
What steps does it require?
How long would it take?
What are its chances of success?
What would happen if it succeeded?

In summary:

In order to Pre-Read a chapter or an assignment, your child follows three steps:

1. He checks the chapter signposts.
2. He uses them to pull out the main thoughts of the chapter.
3. He turns those main ideas into questions.

He does this by placing the words *what, why, where, when, how,* or *who* in front of the thoughts.

And when he has turned them into questions in this way, he then reads the text to answer those questions, and skims over everything else.

Let us now see how he slashes through that text, mastering its content, without repetition, in a single flash reading.

CHAPTER 9

HOW TO POWER-READ—MASTER AN ASSIGNMENT IN MINUTES

Your child has now finished his quick survey of the chapter. He has pulled out its main thoughts and turned them into questions. He is now ready to read the text, word by word, to answer these questions.

Let's see how he does this, in the shortest possible time, without missing a single vital point.

HOW TO DOUBLE YOUR CHILD'S READING RATE

Always, of course, our first goal is to improve your child's ability to understand everything he reads. But this search for understanding does *not* conflict with a second vital goal—to speed up your child's reading rate.

Fast readers are good readers. And most children who read slowly do so because of one or two crippling habits they've picked up in the first or second grade. Eliminate those habits and you liberate tremendous new-reading speed in your child overnight.

Since your child will be faced with a flood of paperwork in his lifetime, *now* is the time to build in that speed. Here are five simple tricks that will do it for him automatically:

1. Don't let your child *point out* the words with his finger or a pencil. This slows him up. Have him read *with his eyes only*. This means his hands must be folded till he turns to the next page.

2. Keep your child from moving his lips or his mouth. Lip moving slows reading speed down to speaking speed. If it's difficult for him to stop moving his lips, have him bite a pencil while he reads till he loses the habit.

93

3. Don't let him move his head from side to side. This tires him out and again slows up his reading. *Only his eyes should move. Only his eyes need to move.*

4. Teach him to read aggressively. Actively. Tearing the ideas out of the pages with the techniques we are showing him in this book.

5. Teach him the habit of skimming and then concentrating as described below. Make every reading assignment a search for main thoughts through a forest of useless words. Let him skim through 90 per cent of those words, and concentrate only on the vital 10 per cent.

And then have him practice. Practice—practice—practice. Till he becomes an expert. Till these habits become second nature. Till he can zip through any written page, anywhere. Like this.

HOW TO FLASH-READ. CUT THROUGH UNIMPORTANT DETAILS IN SECONDS

Now with these speed-reading skills firmly implanted in your child's mind as automatic habits, he begins to attack the chapter, word by word.

He begins to read as fast as he can. He reads every word. *But now he is sifting those words—judging them—accepting them or rejecting them.*

He is looking for specific answers to specific questions—the questions he constructed in his quick survey before he began to read.

These questions are burned into his mind:

What is the definition of a declarative sentence?

How did the forces of nature help shape Greek civilization?

How can my firm cut raw materials costs?

Every word, every phrase, every sentence that his eye flashes over is judged by whether they answer or do not answer those questions.

If they answer the question, he stops, concentrates, underlines as shown below.

If they do not answer the questions, he reads on, searching for his answers.

In this way, he merely skims over 90 per cent of the text—the unimportant 90 per cent—the excess details, the side issues, the interesting opinions and prejudices that will never be asked for in a test.

He reads them all quickly, once. He skips none of them. He lets them register in his brain as they will. He lets them fill in the details of the vital points he will later concentrate on. He makes no deliberate conscious effort to memorize any of them.

But—because at the same time he is building up a structure of one vital thought in the chapter after another—he will find that these skimmed-over details, somehow automatically, stick to these main thoughts.

He will find that he remembers far more of this chapter —main thoughts and details both—than he has ever remembered before.

The reason for this increase in memory is simple. We remember what we can understand and what we can organize. If we try to memorize nonsense words or jumbled sentences, for example, we find it almost impossible. And, to your child, a chapter that is not broken down into main thoughts and details is really nothing but a meaningless jumble.

But once he picks out its main thoughts and puts them in order, he has constructed a *memory framework.* From that moment on he has a logical structure, a definite pigeonhole, for details to attach themselves to in his memory.

Then, even though he skims over these details and concentrates only on consciously memorizing his main thoughts, *the details logically stick along to their parent thoughts, and he gets them in his mind as a sort of no-work bor.*

So he has now flash-read 90 per cent of the chapter—

simply glanced at the details to pick them up—and he is now ready to go to work on his main thoughts.

Here's how he does it.

THE MAGIC KEY TO CONCENTRATION

As you remember, your child is reading to find specific answers to specific questions. Every sentence he reads is judged on that basis. Does it answer his questions, or does it not?

If it does not, he flash-reads it, and searches on for his answers.

If it does, however, he slows down, concentrates his full attention on that sentence, *and picks up his pencil to underline the answer.*

This deliberate physical act—this aggressive underlining of answers in the textbook as they are read—is the Golden Rule that makes your child's concentration automatic.

It converts routine reading into active, physical thought. It prevents his mind from wandering. It makes the dead, lifeless material in the book come to life with the thrill of personal discovery. It forces him to evaluate, weed out, judge, emphasize. It is the first great step in turning that material into *his own personal acquisition* as he hammers it out, answer by answer by answer.

And it is as easy as ABC. There is only one simple procedure to follow.

Every time your child finds the answer to one of his questions, he simply:

a. *Reads it carefully.*

b. *Makes sure he understands it. And*

c. *Underlines once the specific words he's going to use to remember it.*

That's all there is to it. On an entire page he may underline only one or two sentences. In a complete lesson, he may make only four or five marks in his book.

But these physical marks are his own personal mile-stones along the road to mastery of that lesson. They are the first active step, not only to *locating* the vital thoughts of that chapter, *but to making those thoughts part of his mental inventory for as long as he wishes to use them.*

Let's see how this underlining process takes place. Let's put it to work on each of our three sample chapters.

HOW TO POWER-READ THE FIRST SAMPLE CHAPTER

Let's take the first paragraph of the first sample chapter. Here's how it now stands in the textbook:

"A declarative sentence makes a statement. It is followed by a period."

Here's how it should look when your child has finished reading it:

"A declarative sentence <u>makes a statement</u>. It is followed by a period."

He has underlined four words and weeded out the rest. He now knows the first kind of sentence and its definition. He has answered his first question. He now goes on to the second, and the third, and the fourth, till he has finished the lesson.

HOW TO POWER-READ THE SECOND SAMPLE CHAPTER

In this chapter, let's take paragraph 17 as our example. Here's how it now stands in the textbook:

"The Greek homeland, however, had one great geographical advantage: its situation encouraged navigation, even by the rather timid. The irregular coasts of the mainland and the islands provided sheltered anchorages; destructive storms seldom occurred during the long summer, the great season of navigation; and the vessels could go for hundreds of miles without ever losing sight of land. Travel in ships propelled by sails or oars or a combination of the two was cheaper, swifter and more comfortable than an up-

hill and down-dale journey overland. The Greeks, conse-
quently, built up an active maritime trade."

As you remember, your child's Pre-Reading survey had
already established the question he was searching for in this
section. Here is that question:

*How did navigable waters help shape Greek civiliza-
tion?*

With that question in mind, here is how this same para-
graph should look when your child has finished reading it:

"The Greek homeland, however, had one great geo-
graphical advantage: its situation encouraged navigation,
even by the rather timid. The irregular coasts of the main-
land and the islands provided sheltered anchorages; destruc-
tive storms seldom occurred during the long summer, the
great season of navigation; and the vessels could go for
hundreds of miles without ever losing sight of land. Travel
in ships propelled by sail or oars or a combination of the
two was cheaper, swifter and more comfortable than an up-
hill and down-dale journey overland. The Greeks, conse-
quently, built up an active maritime trade."

He has underlined eight words, and weeded out the
rest. These eight words answer his question completely—
allow him to realize that *the navigable waters surrounding
Greece enabled the Greeks to build up an active maritime
trade.* This is the main thought of this paragraph. The rest
is merely detail.

And so he continues with his reading, using this same
technique to weed out 95 per cent of the unimportant words
in the chapter; to concentrate only on the answers to his
main-thought questions; and to build up, answer by answer,
the complete, easily remembered Main Thought Outline of
this lesson, which we will examine in the next chapter.

HOW TO POWER-READ THE THIRD SAMPLE CHAPTER

As a contrast, let's take paragraph 24 of this chapter.
Here's how it stands in the textbook:

"The fifth avenue of cost reduction consists of analysis of general and administrative expenses. In the normal company these cover such items as salaries of executives and office employees, office expenses, interest, property depreciation, taxes, insurance, donations, legal fees, consultants, investigations of possible mergers, economic services and other general business expenses."

As you remember, the question we were using here was:

How can my firm cut general and administrative costs?

With that question in mind, here is how this same paragraph looks when your child has finished it:

"The fifth avenue of cost reduction consists of analysis of general and administrative expenses. In the normal company these cover such items as salaries of executives and office employees, office expenses, interest, property depreciation, taxes, insurance, donations, legal fees, consultants, investigations of possible mergers, economic services and other general business expenses."

Here the answer to the question gives eleven or more ways to cut costs in this area, and all are underlined. Later, when he builds his Main Thought Outline, your child will combine several of them so they can be more easily memorized.

At the present point, however, he continues to read on until he has finished the chapter, answered each of his questions and thoroughly understands each of its main points.

In summary:

Once your child has made his Pre-Reading survey, with its questions to be answered, the actual reading of the lesson becomes incredibly fast and easy.

During this reading, he will skim over about 90 per cent of the text, searching only for the answers to his main-thought questions, and letting their details stick to his memory automatically.

And when he finds a main-thought answer, he actively underlines it, marking each word that he will use later to remember it by.

In this way, he actively builds up a series of main-thought answers, *which he will now use to build a Main Thought Outline in his notebook so he can remember them as long as he wishes.*

It is to this last step of rewriting and remembering that we now turn.

CHAPTER 10

Your child is now ready for the pay-off, the moment when he masters the meaning of the chapter and makes it his own.

What has he done so far? All this:

1. Picked out the main thoughts of the chapter.

2. Turned them into questions.

3. Weeded out material that did not answer those questions, and which he will never have to look at again.

4. Located the answers to those questions—the vital information that composes the backbone of that book.

5. Marked that vital information separate from the rest of the chapter.

He now has everything he needs to know about every main thought in that chapter right at his fingertips. *Now he has to fit them together.*

Now he rewrites the chapter, in his own personal language, making fifty words do the work of five thousand.

HIS NOTEBOOK. WHERE HE RE-CREATES THE BACKBONE MEANING OF EACH CHAPTER, EACH BOOK, EACH COURSE

In addition to his own mind, your child has only three basic tools to open up the entire world of knowledge to his grasp:

His textbook.
His pencil.
And his notebook.

In fact, his grades in school may very well depend on his ability to transfer knowledge from one of these books to the other.

What exactly *is* this notebook of his? What should it contain? How should it be arranged? How exactly does he use it to get the maximum benefit from his reading?

Let's look at each of the points in turn.

Your child's notebook is the actual storehouse of all that he has learned, from every one of his courses, during an entire school semester.

That notebook should be large and loose-leafed. It should have a durable hard cover. It should have plastic colored separators for each course. It should have his name, address, and telephone number written in ink inside the front cover, because it is much too valuable to lose.

Your child should carry this notebook with him every day, to every class. When he sits down at his study table at home at night, it should be the first book he opens. It is his portable organizer. It sets up his entire study schedule, in this way:

Each course in the notebook must be set off by a plastic colored separator. The first page following that separator is the assignment page for that course. On that page, each assignment for each day is copied down exactly as it is given by his teacher, like this:

April 3, 1963

Chapter 2: "Five Roads to Cost Reduction." Pages 64 to 69. Answer questions 1 to 8 at end of chapter, to hand in tomorrow.

Each day's assignments are written in this way on the assignment page, one after another. As they are completed, they are checked off with a red pencil. But they are kept in the notebook, to serve as part of the flash review he will make before he takes any test.

HOW YOUR CHILD WRITES UP EACH
DAY'S LESSON IN HIS NOTEBOOK

After the assignment page, for each course, come the Main Thought Outline pages he will write up, day after day, as he masters that course.

These pages are not haphazard in any way. They are not written in the classroom, not written while he is actually reading the text. There is no room on them for illegible scrawls, written daydreaming, or doodles of any kind.

They are carefully and precisely prepared, in this way:

1.   When your child has finished reading the chapter, and when he has underlined the answers to the main-thought questions that he had previously prepared, he then closes the book.

2.   He is now ready to put his knowledge of the backbone of that chapter to its first test. To do this, he takes a blank sheet of paper—not in his notebook—and from memory he writes down each of the main thoughts of that chapter and the information he has learned about them.

3.   He will forget some of these points. He will write down some of them out of order. He will find that he still doesn't clearly understand some of the information about them. None of this is important. What is important is the fact that he has just made his first recitation, taken his first self test on that chapter.

4.   He now goes back to the text and checks and corrects his outline. He writes the corrections directly onto that rough outline.

5.   When he has finished it, when he has it boiled down and correctly arranged to his own satisfaction, then he turns that paper over. He opens his notebook. And he writes that outline—again from memory—on one page of that notebook.

6.   What he is doing is freeing himself, step by step, from the crutch of that textbook. He is transferring knowledge out of that textbook into his own memory, and then

into his notebook for instant reference. And each step of the way he is condensing that knowledge, memorizing and re-memorizing it, understanding it more deeply and clearly with each word he writes.

7. When he has finished writing the outline in his notebook, he checks it again. If there are one or two errors or omissions, he writes them in. If there are too many, he rewrites the entire page. He writes on only one side of the paper, however, because he will use the other side later to double the profit he gets out of every hour of review.

And then, when he has the outline in his notebook finished to his satisfaction, he closes both books and is finished for the night. He has learned his chapter. He has the backbone of that chapter stored in his memory and his notebook, ready to go to work for him at an instant's notice.

And he can show it to you, in black and white, every night you ask for it in your five-minute Achievement Check. Let's see what these finished outlines should look like, for each one of our three sample chapters, when your child proudly displays them in his notebook.

THE FINISHED OUTLINE FOR OUR FIRST SAMPLE CHAPTER

THE FOUR KINDS OF SENTENCES:

1. *Declarative—makes a statement.*
2. *Interrogative—asks something.*
3. *Exclamatory—shows surprise or excitement.*
4. *Imperative—gives a command.*

THE FINISHED OUTLINE FOR OUR SECOND SAMPLE CHAPTER

THE GREEKS, I. THE BACKGROUND.

1. *Aegean Civilization.*
    Centered at Crete, Troy, Mycenae.
    Contributions were:

a. *Copper and bronze basis for high civilization.*

b. *Advanced engineering techniques produced fortifications and palaces.*

c. *Ruled by kings.*

d. *Empire building through trade and warfare by sea.*

2. *Geographical Influences:*

Poor soil and climate forced Greeks to seek their fortunes overseas.

Easy navigability made sea transportation easier and more profitable than land.

Rough terrain encouraged individual city-states.

THE FINISHED OUTLINE FOR OUR THIRD SAMPLE CHAPTER

FIVE ROADS TO COST REDUCTION.

1. *Cut raw materials cost by:*

a. *Precise purchasing specifications.*

b. *Inspection of incoming materials.*

c. *Elimination of manufacturing difficulties due to raw materials.*

d. *Substitution or elimination of unnecessary materials.*

e. *Financial control of sources.*

2. *Cut capital equipment costs by:*

a. *Reducing costs of depreciation, replacement, maintenance and interest.*

b. *Holding down inventories.*

c. *Sharpening accounting procedures.*

3. *Cut manufacturing costs by:*

a. *Better labor management.*

b. *Analysis of indirect costs.*

c. *Design of new equipment.*

d. *Better working conditions.*

  e. *Improved materials handling.*
  f. *Operations research.*
 4. *Cut sales costs by cutting costs of:*
  a. *Warehousing.*
  b. *Transportation.*
  c. *Advertising.*
  d. *Packaging.*
  e. *Direct sales costs.*
  f. *New specialist costs.*
 5. *Cut general and administrative costs:*
  a. *Administrative salaries.*
  b. *Office expense.*
  c. *Interest.*
  d. *Insurance.*
  e. *Donations.*
  f. *Legal fees.*
  g. *Consultants and other economic services.*

TIPS ON IMPROVING YOUR CHILD'S OUTLINES

 1. Simplify. Keep compressing, boiling down, making the outline shorter and shorter. Use phrases instead of sentences. Eliminate unnecessary words and details. Blend subordinate sentences into others by boiling them down into one or two words. Keep cutting till each idea stands sharp and clear in a few easy-to-remember words.

 2. Fit the ideas together properly. Make sure one leads into the other in the right order. Then, when your child thinks of the first idea, the second automatically pops into his mind.

 3. What are the kinds of order your child can use to make one idea fit in with another? Here are a few:

   A. Parts of Something.

Example:

Kinds of birds:

  1. *Sparrow.*

2. *Robin.*
3. *Bluebird, etc.*

B.   Time Order.

Example:

Battles of World War II:
   1. *Poland.*
   2. *Holland.*
   3. *France.*
   4. *Britain, etc.*

C.   Step-by-Step Sequence.

Example:

How to Build a Model Airplane:
   1. *Check each part and arrange in order.*
   2. *Read instructions carefully.*
   3. *Cut out all parts, etc.*

D.   Causes of Something.

Example:

Causes of 1929 Depression:
   1. *Watered stock.*
   2. *Insufficient government control.*
   3. *Speculation by banks, etc.*

E.   Effects of Something.

Example:

Results of 1929 Depression:
   1. *Vast unemployment.*
   2. *Business bankruptcies.*
   3. *Loss of 1932 election, etc.*

F.   Arrangement by Space.

Example:

States on the Eastern Seaboard:
   1. *Maine.*
   2. *Vermont.*
   3. *New Hampshire.*
   4. *Rhode Island, etc.*

These are only a few samples. Have your child look for other kinds, and keep a list of them at the back of his notebook.

4.   Use numbers. They are a great help, both in understanding a lesson and remembering it for future use. For example, once your child knows that there are *five* roads to cost reduction, he realizes that he must reproduce all five of them on any future test. If he had not numbered them, however, he may have thought there were only four, and left one out because he didn't stop to search for it.

5.   Indent. And then indent again. Physical indentions show instantly the difference between the theme of the entire chapter and its sub-thoughts. And if these sub-ideas have any further divisions, again indentions show their relation at a glance. Notes should be neat and precise, with plenty of white space around each point, so your child can see exactly where it stands in relation to the chapter as a whole when he reviews it.

HOW YOUR CHILD USES HIS NOTES

When your child finishes writing up these notes each night, he has accomplished not one but two vital tasks:

1.   He has read and understood the chapter assigned to him—and understood it more completely than he had ever dreamed before.

2.   He has stored away the backbone meaning of that chapter, *so that he can now thoroughly review it for a test by reading as few as fifty words, instead of as many as five thousand.*

He has two enormous advantages over every other child in his class who does not use this technique. And he begins putting those advantages to use immediately.

His first review takes place right after he finishes those notes, with you in your five-minute Achievement Check that same evening. Here you discover exactly how much your child has gained from his day's reading. Here he accounts to you now—passes your inspection—even before he begins to put this new knowledge to work in his class.

The procedure is simple. You read the notes, then ask questions about any point that seems vague or unclear to you. Then you ask him one or two questions concerning the contents of these notes.

For example, if a point doesn't seem clear to you, ask:

"I don't understand how precise purchasing specifications can cut raw materials cost. Would you mind explaining that to me?"

Or, as an example of a general-review question on the contents of the second sample chapter, ask him:

"How about giving me those three geographical influences again?"

Your child should be able to answer each of these questions instantly from memory, without referring back to his notes. Soon he will look forward to these check periods with tremendous anticipation. And you, on your part, must be sure to show the enthusiasm and pride you feel.

When you are through with the individual chapter notes each evening, then test his over-all mastery of the course by asking him these questions, which force him to tie in his daily reading with everything he has learned before:

"Why do you think the author placed this chapter where it is in the book?"

"How does it tie in with the chapter you read yesterday?"

"What did you have to know in yesterday's chapter before you could understand the material you read today?"

These questions force your child to think. To tie in. To relate forward and backward. And to become accustomed to expressing his thoughts in his own words.

When he is through with that Achievement Check each night, he knows that he has mastered that material. And he's confident that he can talk sense about it to anyone.

THE NEXT MORNING

And the next morning, on his way to class, he takes one more brief look over these notes. Riding to school, walking through the halls, with his notebook closed, he runs through these three magic questions:

"In one sentence, what did I learn from last night's chapter?" (That the five roads to cost reduction are through reducing raw materials costs, manufacturing costs, capital equipment costs, sales costs, and general and administrative costs.)

"How does this tie in with the chapter before?" (It's a second way of increasing profits, right after improved management.)

"What questions will I be asked on it in next week's test?" (To list several ways of reducing costs in each one of these areas. And he runs through them.)

Using this planned technique, in half the time that it would have taken him to read that chapter before, he is now ready to go in that classroom and make his classmates' eyes pop open in amazement.

In summary:

There is an easy, simple, organized way to master the contents of any assignment. It consists of the following three steps:

1. Pre-Read the assignment, to pick out its main thoughts and turn them into questions.

2. Power-read the assignment, to weed out unnecessary details and concentrate on the answers to these questions.

3. Translate the assignment into a Main Thought Outline that expresses these answers in as few words as possible, and that is stored for instant review in your child's notebook.

These are the three Magic Keys to Expert Reading. You should have your child practice them again and again and again, until they become second nature to him. They will pay him dividends for the rest of his life.

CHAPTER 11

THE ALL-IMPORTANT ART OF LISTENING— RIGHT DOWN TO READING THE SPEAKER'S THOUGHTS

In addition to reading, your child gains the information he needs in school by listening.

In fact, in his later life, when he goes into the business and social worlds, his ability to listen well will be even more important than his ability to read well. Most adults gain about 80 per cent of all new facts through their ears, not their eyes.

Therefore hearing everything that is said, and missing nothing, is an indispensable art. *But it is an art. It is not a natural gift. You must teach it to him. Just as he must learn how to read, so he must learn how to listen in this simple but tremendously powerful way:*

HOW TO DEVELOP YOUR CHILD'S LISTENING POWER FROM THE VERY FIRST GRADE

When do you start to develop this ability to listen in your child? The very first moment he can understand a fairy tale or story, and answer questions about it. It may be as early as the age of four or five; it certainly should be no later than his enrollment in the first grade.

Start this way. Some night, at the dinner table if you have a four- or five- or six-year-old, make up a new game. Tell your child that you're going to read him a list of objects —toys, games, the names of his friends, what have you. Then ask him to name back that list in the order in which you gave it to him.

It's as simple as that. Start with a list of ten objects.

Award prizes. See how many he can name, and how much he can improve. At first he'll remember two or three. Then four or five. Then all ten—perfectly.

As he grows older, make the game harder. Tell him a story, and ask him to repeat the important facts. Read him a newspaper article and then ask him questions about it. Try to stick him with specific names and figures. Watch him repeat them back to you, number by number.

You'll be astounded at how much he can retain. And you've taught him the first secret of good listening—strengthening his ear-channel memory—learning to remember everything important that he hears.

Now he's ready for the second step.

HOW TO CONCENTRATE ON THE SPEAKER'S THOUGHTS, AND NEVER BE DISTRACTED

Once your child has strengthened his listening memory, so that he can hold entire thoughts and sentences in his mind after hearing them only once, he's ready to fit them together into meaningful patterns as the speaker talks. There is a definite technique to re-creating the core of a lecture—any lecture—so that he need never forget it. Here's how:

Learning to listen well—to hear everything of real importance that's being said—is primarily a matter of being able to *maintain attention*. Of pacing himself to follow the speaker's thoughts, and not letting his mind wander off. Because of this fact, the power of complete attention has been called the mark of an educated man.

Why is it difficult to maintain this attention? Because the human brain thinks about four times as fast as the human tongue can speak. And the huge gap between the speed of his mind and the words he is hearing provides time for all sorts of distracting personal thoughts.

How does he keep these distracting thoughts from leading him astray? *By forcing himself to keep pace with the* speaker in these three ways, everytime he finds his mind about to wander:

1. *By summarizing what the speaker has already said, and building it into a main-thought outline.* Here he asks himself questions like these:

How can I sum up these statements in a single phrase?

How do they tie in with his last point?

2. *By anticipating the speaker's next point,* with questions like these:

What is he getting at here?

Where will he go now?

What examples must he give to prove this point?

3. *By listening "between the lines" for points that are not put into words,* with questions like these:

What is he implying here?

Why does he stick to this one point, and not go on to the other we were discussing last week?

Is he hinting at more than he's willing to say right out?

And so on, with other questions that will come to your child's mind as he seeks the inner meaning of the speaker's words.

All these questions have one vital trait in common. *They turn listening from a passive to an active occupation.* They stop drifting. They force your child to *think* step by step with the speaker. To keep his mind constantly focused on that speaker's thoughts, both expressed and unexpressed. To literally pull the core meaning out of that lecture as it develops in front of him.

And then, as he does in his reading, night after night, he stores that core meaning on paper so he can have it for good. In this way:

HOW TO TAKE LECTURE NOTES

Your child now has two powerful tools that enable him to capture the inner meaning of any spoken statement, lecture, or conversation he may hear.

He has developed a strong listening memory, so he can hold entire thoughts and sentences in his mind after hearing them only once.

And he has the ability to keep his attention focused on the speaker's thoughts, both expressed and unexpressed, for as long as necessary to pull out the inner meaning of those thoughts as it develops in front of him.

He now makes these two gifts even more effective by learning how to re-create the backbone meaning of that lecture in his own notebook, where he will have it for instant reference whenever he needs it.

Because a word is spoken once and then is lost forever, lecture notes are prepared differently from reading notes. Though the end result is the same, the technique of capturing the main thoughts must work far faster in the lecture hall than in the reading room.

Here is that technique, step by step:

1. The more your child knows about the material covered by a lecture, the more he will get out of that lecture. Therefore he should always read the material in the textbook *before* it's covered in the lecture. Then he can use at least part of the lecture as a review, rather than a new learning experience.

2. What your child is looking for in such a lecture is *enrichment*. This is the material that the teacher includes in his lecture that is *not* in the textbook, and that can never be picked up by mere textbook reading alone. This bonus information should form the core of the lecture, and should be what your child brings home in his notebook.

3. The lecture pages in his notebook should be separate from his reading pages. To begin with, of course, he will take his lecture notes on a piece of scrap paper, where he can jot down ideas as they seem important to him, and cross them out or rearrange them as he sees corrections are necessary. Only after the lecture is over will he write them up in

finished form and put them into his notebook, as we explain below.

4. These lecture notes begin the moment your child walks into the room. He has already reviewed the textbook material he believes will be covered in the lecture; he is prepared to listen. He takes a seat as far forward in the room as possible. He places his book and notebook on the floor, leaving on the desk only a piece of scrap paper and his pen or pencil with which to write.

5. He writes at the top of that paper the date, the name of the lecturer if it is different from his regular teacher, and the subject of the lecture as soon as it is announced.

6. His first goal is to discover the central theme, the main point, the speaker's goal in giving the lecture. He finds this out in one of several ways:

It may be contained in the lecture title. A lecture on *The Five Roads to Cost Reduction*, for example, would give him the theme immediately.

If the title is vague, however, then he must look elsewhere. Perhaps the lecturer distributes notes on mimeographed sheets before the lecture. These should be carefully read and the main thoughts underlined. If the central theme is given on the sheet, it should be transferred to his note paper immediately.

If there are no printed notes, then your child must listen carefully to the lecturer's opening remarks. He should, of course, disregard introductory acknowledgments, anecdotes, jokes, and so on, and concentrate on picking up such *signal phrases* as the following:

"I wish to discuss tonight the problem of——"
"The theme of my lecture tonight will be——"
"Have you ever thought of the extreme importance to this country of——"

Somewhere in these opening remarks, the main theme will emerge. As soon as he has it, it should be boiled down in his mind to one or two phrases, and written at the top of his paper. There it will control the development of his out-line—tell him exactly what to look for in the rest of the lecture.

HOW TO RECOGNIZE THE SPEAKER'S MAIN POINTS

7.   Once he knows the main theme of the lecture, your child's next goal is obvious. He must chart the *development* of that central theme through one vital thought after an-other. He is now building his outline from the speaker's words—listening for main thoughts and writing each of them down in order.

8.   To do this he listens 90 per cent of the time and writes the other ten. Note taking is not stenography. It is never merely writing down the exact words the lecturer uses, even if that were possible. Note taking is condensation. Judgment. Weeding out the unimportant. Boiling down the central thoughts, as they occur, to a few capsule words or phrases, and then fitting them into their place in his growing outline.

9.   How does he recognize these main thoughts? In two ways. First because they are *big ideas* pertaining to the central theme of the lecture. (For example, in a lecture on *The Five Roads to Cost Reduction,* once your child has heard the speaker say, *"Now, the first road to cost reduction is, of course, to cut raw materials costs,"* he would know that he had his first main thought.)

10.   Next, your child recognizes the lecture's main thoughts by the *signal words* the speaker uses to introduce them. These signal words are much like the chapter signposts that guided your child to the meaning of his textbook read-ing. They are verbal signals that flag his attention, that warn him that something really important will follow them. Let's look at a few of them right now.

Any number is a direct give-away that the speaker is going to list his main points for the audience. He may even give the audience advance notice of how many main points he's going to have, in this way:

"*Now, the geographical setting of ancient Greece had three main influences upon Greek civilization.*"

At that point your child marks in his rough notes:
Influences of geographical setting:

1. _____

_____

2. _____

_____

3. _____

_____

He now knows that there are three geographical influences, and he has set aside space for each of the three as they come up in the lecture. He now has a built-in *main-thought trap* in his notes. He listens without writing until the speaker signals him again, by saying: "*The first geographical influence——*"

Then he writes it down, and waits for the second and the third.

These number signals are the most clear-cut clues the speaker will give him to the number and arrangement of his main thoughts. But there are others almost as useful. Here are some of them, and what they tell your child:

That another important fact is coming—*next, then, further, besides, moreover, but, in addition.*

That another important event is taking place in the speaker's time sequence—*then, soon, meanwhile, later, at last, finally.*

That the speaker is going to illustrate a main point by a specific case—*for example, especially, in particular.*

That a new main point is going to be introduced to contrast with the main point that has just been covered—*on the other hand, yet, still, however, on the contrary, but, nevertheless.*

That the lecture is coming to a conclusion (at this point

your child should watch for a summing up that will give him a chance to check and see whether he has all the main points in their right order)—*in conclusion, to sum up, finally, hence, so, thus, as a result.*

And, finally, other signal words to watch for, because they may point up a main thought that follows them, are— *all things considered, above all, for this reason, to this end, likewise, and so.*

HOW THE LECTURER POINTS OUT THE QUESTIONS HE'S GOING TO ASK ON FUTURE TESTS

11. In addition to these automatic signal words that point out the main thoughts of the lecture, the speaker many times will deliberately pause, then tell the class that such and such a point is going to be asked for in a future test. He may use any one of the following forms to announce this:

"It is important to note——"
"Be sure to know——"
"Pay special attention to——"

Or he may come right out and say it:

"You'll be asked to——"
"This will be a test question——"

Once your child hears these clues, he sets this point off from the rest of the lecture in this way. He marks a large TQ (for Test Question) beside it. Then, in his review later on, he can give it special attention.

HOW TO FINISH THE NOTES SO THEY CONTAIN EVERYTHING HE NEEDS FROM THE LECTURE

12. Now, what has your child done so far during this lecture? He has:

written down the central theme at the top of his paper,

jotted down the main headings as they were either outlined for him at the beginning of the lecture, or as they emerged during its development, left plenty of room after each of these headings to serve as main-thought traps to pick up their vital sub-points,

and filtered out these sub-points by careful, active listening, and by following the clues the speaker's signal words gave him.

13. Therefore, at the end of the lecture, your child should have the main-thought backbone of that lecture completely down on his rough sheet of paper. *Now his job is to rewrite those notes into finished form as soon as possible.*

14. If he has the time, he stays in the lecture hall after the other students have left, and rewrites them there. Or in his next classroom, before the class begins, he rewrites them there. In any case, he uses the first available five minutes to fix those notes firmly in his notebook and in his mind.

15. He rewrites them in this way. He rereads everything he has put down on that rough sheet of paper, making sure he understands each point and its relation to every other point in the lecture. Then, if necessary, he puts them in the correct and final order. He weeds out. He numbers. He underscores. He organizes. Until he has these notes written as clearly and completely as his reading notes every night.

16. This is his first self-recitation of the material in this lecture. When he has finished it, and when he has fitted it into place behind his other lecture notes, he has made that lecture his own. He is now ready to relate it to his reading notes on the same material, and put it to use whenever he needs it for class recitation or a test.

TWO OTHER VITAL CLASSROOM TECHNIQUES

At one time or another during a lecture, your child, no matter how bright he is, will have a moment when he just doesn't understand one of the speaker's statements, or when he has a thought that would modify that statement.

Therefore he must get into the habit of asking questions, of speaking up in the classroom as well as at home.

If the teacher allows questions during the lecture, he should ask a brief, polite, to-the-point question immediately. This question should have one purpose: to clear up the point that is vague in his mind. Once it is cleared up, he should write the point and its answer in his rough notes, and check it later to make sure he has understood it. As we shall discuss later, any misunderstanding is a golden opportunity for learning.

If the teacher does not permit questions during the lecture, then your child should speak to him after class. In any case, he should never leave the classroom with the question unanswered.

At the same time, if sample problems are done by the teacher during the lecture, or as part of a homework assignment, your child should copy them, word by word, right into his notebook.

This is essential—especially in his mathematics classes—for these two reasons:

First, because it trains him away from attempting his own short-cut methods, where he may leave out vital steps and get hopelessly lost. And it eliminates the necessity for him to copy answers rather than mastering the methods that produce them.

(In later life, there will be no pat answers to copy. Then only methods will be of any use. And, if he is going to compete, he had darned well better know them.)

And secondly, this step-by-step copying of sample problems is one more way of assuring attentiveness. Again, the best way by far to learn is actively, with a pencil in your hand.

In summary:

Power-listening can be developed as effectively as Power-reading, simply by learning a few easy techniques. These are:

Strengthening your child's listening memory, so he can retain whole phrases, thoughts, and sentences in his mind after hearing them only once.

Teaching him to maintain full concentrated attention on the speaker's words, so that no important thought, expressed or unexpressed, can escape him.

And showing him how to boil a lecture down into its vital thoughts, each in its proper order, so he can store the backbone meaning of that lecture in his mind and his notebook for instant reference whenever he needs it.

CHAPTER 12

HOW YOUR CHILD CAN GET TWICE AS MUCH
OUT OF HIS DAILY READING

Now let's put these reading skills to work for your child in another area.

Let's see how they can save him time and effort every single day. Double the amount of information he gets out of a magazine or newspaper. Cut his daily reading time in half. Let him flash right through Shakespeare or Dickens, and dazzle his class that very next morning with the insights he has into every one of its events and characters.

Let's start with the Number One source of information for most people—the newspaper:

HOW THE PROFESSIONALS READ THEIR
NEWSPAPER

He needs two separate skills—two separate patterns of action—to get the most out of his daily paper:

1. How to read his newspaper as a whole.

2. How to read each individual news story that catches his eye.

First, let's set up an over-all pattern of attack—a timed, step-by-step procedure—that will help him tear out all the important facts from his paper every evening or morning.

Here's how he does it—step by step:

1. When he opens his newspaper in the morning, the first thing he does is skim all the headlines on the front page. (Or, if your house reads a tabloid, he should skim all the headlines of the first four or five pages.)

What he is trying to achieve here—with this first rapid, over-all view of the headlines—is "to see the world in one piece." To get a bird's-eye view of all the important events of the day at one time. *And to see—if possible—how each of these events ties in to all the others.*

For example, consider the fateful week of October 12, 1964. Scanning the typical newspaper of any day that week, he would see that the Labor government has just been elected in England . . . that Khrushchev had been pushed out of the Soviet government . . . that Red China had exploded an atomic bomb . . . that Johnson and Goldwater were battling for the presidency of the United States.

Now, what does this bird's-eye view show him? First of all—change! Country after country is changing internally. And the balance of power of the world itself is changing externally. *But exactly how? How rapidly? Towards what?*

How do these events tie in to each other? What is the connection between Khrushchev's fall from power and the Chinese bomb? What effect will both these events have on the American election?

This first two-minute glance tells him what happened on that day, and leads him to set up questions in his mind about why it happened, and what effect one event will have on the other. He now reads to answer these questions. He does it in this way:

HOW TO READ A NEWS STORY

2. Now he starts on the articles themselves. His objective here is to get the big facts—the important facts—out of each story as fast as he can, without missing a single vital detail.

He does this by going back to the headline, and turning it into a series of questions. For example:

KHRUSHCHEV REMOVED FROM POWER

brings these questions to mind:

Why?

How?

By whom?

What was done with him?

What will happen next?

Or this headline:

RED CHINA EXPLODES A-BOMB

brings these questions to mind:

How big was it?

How powerful?

How many does China have?

Was it a real bomb, or just a test device?

Does China have the means to drop it overseas?

What will happen next?

Now—with these questions in mind—he reads the first paragraph of the story. The first paragraph is actually a *complete summary* of the story. It gives him an outline of what follows. It should answer most of his questions—along with Who? . . . What? . . . When? . . . Where? . . . Why? . . . and How?

Now, in most stories, this first (or second, or third) paragraph should give him as much information as he wants to know. In other words, it should answer his questions— at least in outline form.

However, if he wishes to gain more information on any one of these points, he reads on. Each of the paragraphs that follow should be an expansion of one of the main points summarized in the first paragraph. He skims each paragraph till he finds that point mentioned again, and then reads it carefully to pick up the details he wants.

This way, there is no waste reading, and no waste time.

He simply:

    1. Reads the headline.

    2. Frames the questions he wants answered about the details in that story.

    3. Reads the first one or two paragraphs to answer those questions.

    4. And then reads on only to pick up details on those points which vitally interest him.

By using this system he can get the guts of a story in a minute or two. And then he's ready to go on and

LEARN THE BACKGROUND BEHIND THE NEWS

    3. Now—when he's read the important news of the day, and its important details—he now turns to the sections of your paper that tell him:

What does it all mean?

Now he gets the comment of skilled interpreters to unravel this news and help him with his own opinions. So he next reads the columnists whose job it is to assign meanings to these events.

And then he turns to the editorial pages where the paper itself interprets the news and takes stands on the major issues of the day. And where readers like himself air their reactions in their letters to the editors.

Now—how does he pull out the gist of these many interpretations in only a few minutes each day? By reading them like this:

An editorial is built up differently from a news story. In a news story the conclusion comes first; the details later. In an editorial, however, the writer begins by reciting facts you already know—by reviewing the situation to make it fresh in your mind. And then he goes on to state his own conclusion. Or solution. Or what he wants you to think and do.

So your child always reads a column or editorial backwards. He reads the last paragraph first, to see if he can't pick up the writer's final interpretation.

Then he jumps to the front. Skims rapidly through the first paragraphs. Looks only for background facts that he doesn't know . . . reasons to support his interpretation . . . what the writer thinks will happen next.

Only a few minutes for each column, and he's through with the main news of the day. But look what he's accomplished! *He's not only got the facts down solid, but has formed his own opinions, and got plenty of good, solid, clearly-thought-through ideas to back them up!*

With this technique, he'll never be at sea in a serious discussion again. He'll know exactly where he stands on important issues. He'll think straight on crucial decisions—lead his classmates opinions on issue after issue.

AND NOW HE GOES ON TO FINISH THE PAPER

4. Now he turns to the index. Reviews the minor stories. Picks out the subjects of special interest to him—sports, business, fashion, home, what have you.

He uses the same headline—question—answer technique on each story he glances at. Pulls out the facts he wants—in minutes.

If he reads movie or stage or book reviews, he uses the same last-paragraph-first technique that he used on the editorials. He gets the conclusion first. Then fills in whatever details interest him.

5. And when he's through with the paper, he just doesn't throw it away and forget it. He thinks of the news as a continued story. Follows each story as it develops day by day. Always—*tries to anticipate what will happen next.*

6. If he can, have him read at least two different papers a day. Try to get different viewpoints in each. Compare them.

Find out where they differ. Sharpen his reasoning power. Judge for himself which one is right.

7. And, of course, have him supplement his papers with radio, TV, lectures, books, etc.

Let's see how he puts one of these "bonus media" to work—in half the time he's using today.

HOW TO FLASH-READ MAGAZINES

With magazines, his plan of attack is different. Here's how he reads them most efficiently:

1. He starts with the Table of Contents. Checks off the articles that interest him most. Turns their titles into questions, and then turns to them.

2. He reads each article's title and subtitle . . . the first paragraph . . . all subheads . . . and the last paragraph or two. This should give him the main idea, and enough information to tell him whether he wants to read further or not.

3. If he does go further, again he asks questions before he reads word by word. Remember—magazines present more than mere fact; they also give opinion. So, if he comes across this kind of headline:

A PLAN TO FREE CUBA

He asks himself these questions:
What is it?
Who is its author?
How qualified is he?
What steps does his plan require?
How long would it take?
What are its chances of success?
What would happen if it succeeded?

4. Also, remember that most magazine articles are trying to get him to *feel, believe,* or *do* something. Therefore,

he asks himself:

> What reaction does this author want from me?
> How does he try to convince me that I should do this?
> What facts or arguments does he use to do this?
> What facts does he distort?
> What facts does he leave out?
> Where can I get the other side of this proposal?

5. To help him answer that last question, try to get him to read at least two magazines—with as contrasting viewpoints as possible. Have him compare their interpretations. See what facts one leaves out that the other stressed. Form his own judgments.

6. Now he skims through the article. Skips details. Gets the main thoughts. Goes on till he's answered his questions. And then turns to the next article.

7. When he's finished the main articles of interest, then he quickly skims through the magazine, page by page. He may pick up something of interest that wasn't fully disclosed in the Table of Contents.

8. To read fiction in magazines, as in books, he follows these rules:

HOW TO READ FICTION TWICE AS FAST, AND REMEMBER TWICE AS MUCH

1. Remember—*all fiction is about people*. Therefore, his first job is to get acquainted with the *people* in his book. He asks himself: Who is the hero? Then writes his name on the inside front cover of the book. Describes him—his appearance and his character.

Who is the heroine? He writes her name. Describes her. Jots down the character traits and desires that are going to determine her actions throughout the book.

Who is the villain? He describes him. Lists his motives. Tells why they're going to bring him in conflict with the hero.

Where are they all? He makes sure he knows the time and location of their surroundings.

What are they trying to do? What blocks them from doing it? *What's going to happen next?*

2. He then reads the *first* chapters carefully. They set the stage—forecast the ultimate outcome. Then he can read faster and faster as the characters become more familiar—as the action becomes more predictable.

3. He tries to outguess the author. The author has planted hints on what's going to happen at the end. Can your child predict that end before the author tells it to him. If your child can, he'll not only get a tremendous kick out of it, but he'll learn how to see into people—predict what they'll do under stress. And this is the great benefit he's looking for from great fiction.

4. When he reaches the end, he asks: What happened? To whom? How did they change—for better or for worse?

What is the author trying to say? What moral is he pointing out? What kind of world does he say it is?

Is it true to life? Does your child believe in the characters—in the events—in the outcome? This is the ultimate test. When he's answered this question, he's told himself whether he's just read great fiction, or pulp fiction.

And finally, what has he learned? What has this author, in this book, taught your child about the way human beings act, feel, believe, fight, love, build and even die!

Never fool yourself. Your child can learn easily as much from fiction as he can from fact. And he can put these new insights . . . these new emotions . . . these new competencies in handling people—to work for him, the very same day!

5. Now, if possible, he reads the reviews or his textbook criticisms. Compares their judgments with his. Searches for the *reasons* these reviewers give for their judgments. Then sees if his reasons hold up as well. If not, he revises and strengthens them.

6. And now he turns to the back cover of the book. Sums up the entire book in one paragraph. Who did what—against what obstacles—and with what results? He tries to boil down the entire experience—the entire moral—into one brief summary that will unlock the entire book for him again if he comes back to it even a year later.

FOR ADVANCE STUDENTS: HOW TO READ BUSINESS ARTICLES AND TECHNICAL REPORTS

Business articles and technical reports have three main purposes:

To report on work in progress.

To detail particulars of some specific operation or method.

To describe new and modern approaches to the problems of the profession or field.

Therefore, to keep up with his field (or to conduct out-of-class research) with the least possible expenditure of time, he reads them this way:

1. With a business journal, he follows the same first step as he did when reading any other kind of magazine. He reads the Table of Contents first. Marks the articles of interest. Reads their summaries. Then decides if he'll read them thoroughly.

2. In reading a technical report, however, he must always define his *purpose* first. He must tell himself exactly why he's reading it. Exactly what he's looking for. Then he must disregard everything else.

3. Don't let him be fooled by their formidable appearance. Their organization is usually quite simple. First he reads the title. Then looks for a summary—usually in the first paragraphs or the last.

4. He disregards footnotes. In nine cases out of ten, they're only for specialists.

5. He concentrates on getting the main ideas. Numbers them. If the report describes a new procedure, he looks for each important step. Numbers them.

6. He should be able to boil down each report, each article, into a main-idea summary no longer than an index card. (If he wants to keep the details, then he saves the article. Files it with reference to the index card.)

After he's boiled it down, he turns the index card over and tries to repeat its contents to himself from memory. He tries to get every numbered point in the proper sequence. This gives him a stronger grip on the article's organization—burns it main points into his memory.

7. *Now he decides what to do with that information.* Should he put it to work. Use it in a report at once. File it for future research. New information means new ability—new power—new competence. In the long run—if it's put to use—it means future prestige and new money when he leaves school and begins to carve a career of his own!

In summary:

Your child can double the amount of reading he gets done every day—and remember twice as much of it—if he follows these simple rules:

1. *Look before he leaps.* Get the main idea first. Don't start reading word-by-word till he knows it.

2. *Ask questions.* Read to answer them. Stop reading when he's got their answers.

3. *Skip details.* They'll only confuse him while he's reading—slip out of his mind as soon as he closes the page. He must concentrate on the core. Number it. Memorize it.

4. *Then put it to work.* Remember—new knowledge means new opportunity—in school, and out of it.

PART THREE

EXPRESSING THE FACTS—WRITING AND RECITING

CHAPTER 13

The most evident and measurable product that your child sells in school is the daily paper he writes. The appearance of the papers that he hands in to his teachers will, in their minds, be just as much a part of him as the clothes he wears. Therefore they should be given just as much thought and attention by his parents.

But this kind of care—neatness and precision on every single paper he hands in—pays one other huge dividend. *It will automatically, by itself alone, eliminate about 20 per cent of the errors sloppiness would otherwise force him into.*

It will eliminate mistakes in addition, subtraction, multiplication, and division that might otherwise cost him downgrading from an "A" to a "B." We will discuss this in detail in our section on mathematics.

It will eliminate mistakes in English, history, social studies, and other compositions that might irritate his teacher so much that she could no longer concentrate on the content of his paper, and thus mark his work on the basis of his weaknesses rather than his strengths.

Yes, if you can permanently install a sense of neatness, precision, and correctness in your child, you can boost his grades a full 20 per cent. *And it is so incredibly simple to do.*

The procedure is a cinch. It consists of three steps:

1. A check on his present papers, to detect his major penmanship errors.

2. The correction of these errors by practicing the correct way to do what he's doing wrong today.

3. And a constant, brief-glance check every night, to see that the old errors don t creep back in.

Now, leaving neatness in mathematics to a later chapter, let's examine the most common penmanship errors your child might make today, and see how easy it is to correct them.

THE THIRTEEN FATAL ERRORS IN PENMANSHIP, AND HOW TO CORRECT THEM

1. *Fails to dot his i's or cross his t's.*
Example:

The dog hit its right toe

How to Correct: Just use perseverance. Make sure **every i and t**, in every word, is finished off correctly.

2. *Has irregular slant.*
Example:

slanted wrong

How to Correct: Use the following slant guide under your child's writing paper until he automatically slants each letter correctly.

3. *Spacing is uneven.*
Example:

spacing uneven

How to Correct: Insist on a space equal to the width of a small letter between words. Don't allow him to crowd the letters in each word together. There should be white space showing between every two letters.

4. *His letters are irregular in size.*
Example:

Letters are irregular

How to Correct: All small letters should be exactly the same size and height, with capitals and loop letters twice as high. To instill this habit, have your child write on lined paper, like the following, till it becomes second nature to him.

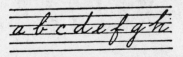

5. *He writes uphill or downhill.*
Example:

writes uphill or downhill

How to Correct: Again, use ruled paper to control wandering, until the habit of writing in a straight line becomes automatic.

writes uphill or downhill

6. *His loop letters are too thin or too fat.*
Example:

His loop letters

How to Correct: Loops should be open, but no wider than an ordinary small letter. Long stems should be kept straight and not curved, as shown in the next example.

7. *His stems are not straight.*
Example:

His stems are not straight

How to Correct: Stems are the backbone or straight downward strokes, which are part of most letters. They should be written as slanted parallel lines, like this:

ϕ ϕ ϕ g h f f k l

8. *He doesn't close his letters.*
Example:

He doesn't close

How to Correct: Letters must be closed carefully at all places indicated by the arrows below. There should be no open spaces at all.

ǒ d̆ a̓ ᶊ ğ ᵏ ᵍ̌ ᶠ

9. *He makes pointed letters where they should be round.*
Example:

The wind machine is mine

How to Correct: Letters like m, n, v, u, h, and y have rounded tops or bottoms. They should not come to a point. To correct, have your child slow up a little when he comes to such letters.

10. *He does not retrace properly.*
Example:

t m i u d

How to Correct: Retracing means carefully writing over a part of the letter that your child has made before. Worst offenders are d and t. See that each retracing looks like a single line.

11. *His endings are too individual.*
Example:

g d s y p z

How to Correct: Make sure his endings come no higher than those of a small letter, and eliminate any unnecessary curves in them.

12. *He makes sloppy capital letters.*
Example:

Capital Letters Give Me

How to Correct: There are several styles of good capital letters. Have your child select one of them and stick to it, until he can write that style simply and well. Remember, fancy flourishes went out with the nineteenth century.

13. *He writes his lines in a slanting column.*
Example:

When in the course of human events it becomes necessary for a people to sever the economical and political bonds connecting it to another people, and affirm before God the

How to Correct: Place a rule down the left-hand column of the page, and have him make sure that every first word in every line touches it.

In all of these common errors, *practice* is the only sure cure. With practice, and careful checking on your part, your child will develop the habit of neatness and precision. And with precision, higher grades must automatically follow.

In summary:

Neatness and penmanship are the first requirements of the successful student. They breed correctness. And correctness alone can improve your child's grades by as much as 20 per cent.

To improve your child's neatness and penmanship, adopt this simple three-step procedure:

1. Check his present work, to detect errors.
2. Correct those errors by practice in doing them the right way.
3. Recheck each night, to guard against errors creeping back in.

We will now see how the same procedure, plus a fascinating trick, can wipe out spelling errors almost overnight.

CHAPTER 14

CORRECT SPELLING MADE EASY

In later life, when your son is submitting a résumé for an important job, or your daughter is writing an application for membership in a club, a single mistake in spelling can ruin the entire impression either is trying to make.

There is no passing grade in spelling beneath 100 per cent. It must be perfect. And it can be, if your child is taught to follow these simple rules:

THE WRONG AND RIGHT WAYS
TO IMPROVE HIS SPELLING

In the first place, *don't* try to improve his spelling by asking him to go over lists of misspelled words and correct them. These lists only concentrate his attention on the *wrong* spelling.

Instead, focus his efforts on the *right* spelling, in the *right* way, like this:

Realize that the reason your child misspells any word is because he has a *distorted image* of that word in his mind. Your job is to help him get rid of that distorted image, and replace it with the correct one in such a way that it is burned forever into his memory.

You do this in three simple steps:

First, you make him *see* that word in such a way that *the correct spelling of the hard part of the word* sticks out like a sore thumb.

Second, you give him *spell-alikes* for the hard part of the word that brings the right spelling of it automatically to his mind everytime.

And third, you have him write that word *twice as large*

as he ordinarily writes, until he gets the correct *feel* of the word forever implanted in the muscles of his arm.

Not only are these three correction steps simple and easy, they are also enormous fun. Let's see how each of them works:

STEP ONE: *SEE* THE HARD PART OF THE WORD CORRECTLY

As you know, most words that are misspelled are misspelled in only one place in the entire word. Either your child has added a letter where it shouldn't be, or forgotten one where it should be, or put in an *e* for an *a,* or doubled a letter when it should remain single, or some other simple mistake.

But, once he has developed that distorted image of the word, then it sticks in his mind. He misspells that word over and over again, always in the same way, always in the same place.

From that moment on, there is a part of that word that your child automatically misspells. It is that *hard part* on which you now concentrate.

First, you check over his papers and pick out the misspelled words. Then you locate the hard part of each of those words—the one or two letters in it that he automatically misspells.

And then you rewrite that word correctly—this time CAPITALIZING those hard letters.

You write it like this:

 climB
 boRRow
 UNable
 paraLLel
 tomoRRow
 arGUMent, and so on.

Now, you let your child *see* this capitalized correct

spelling. You ask him to copy the correct spelling on a sheet of paper—*with the capitals in exactly the same place that you have put them.*

Have him write that word over and over and over again —capitals and all—until he's got it down pat. Until he can see the correct capitalized spelling of the hard part of that word *with his eyes shut.*

Then you've completed his first step. He's well on his way to perfect spelling.

STEP TWO: BUILD AN *AUTOMATIC MEMORY PROMPTER* TO SPELL THE HARD PART OF THE WORD CORRECTLY

Now, you are going to reinforce that correct picture image of that word in your child's mind. You are going to do it by giving him a simple *spell-alike* to help him remember how the difficult letters go.

You are going to create an *automatic memory tie-in* between the difficult part of the word and an easy-to-remember spell-alike, like this:

There are three different ways to create these spell-alikes. Try them in the following order, until you get one that your child automatically remembers.

First of all, look for *familiar words within the hard words,* to make them easy to remember. Make up little sentences that tie these familiar words and the hard words together. For example:

"The SECRET was kept by the SECRETary."

"After I ATE, I was grATEful."

"We will GAIN a barGAIN."

"It's VILE to allow special priVILEge."

"Scientists LABOR in a LABORatory."

Second, if there are no familiar words within the hard words, then look for *the same part* in smaller familiar words. For example:

"We write a lettER on our stationERy."

"When we PARt, we sePARate."

"Please BRing the umBRella."

Finally, if neither of these first two rules works, then make up pure spell-alikes for your child—as funny and as nonsensical as possible. For example:

"She screamed EEE as she passed the cEmEtEry."

"The RR train and I had a quaRRel."

"GM uses good judGMent."

"I gave HER HER handKERchief."

"I say BR when I think of FeBRuary."

There is a spell-alike for every misspelled word. One of these three rules will turn up the right one for your child. Remember, keep them as vivid and as funny as possible; in that way, they'll be much easier to remember.

And, once your child is on to the game, let him think up the spell-alikes. It's not only great fun to see who can come up with the most outlandish ones, but it's marvelous training for future creativity.

And, always, it makes the correct spelling of those difficult words *automatic,* as soon as the spell-alike flashes into his mind to tell him the way those hard letters should go.

STEP THREE: GET THE *ARM-FEEL* OF WRITING THAT HARD WORD CORRECTLY

Now, after you've capitalized the hard part of that misspelled word, and after you've both thought up a spell-alike to remember its correct order automatically, then your child is ready to *build the correct spelling of the word into a written reflex* without his even thinking of it.

Here's how:

Give your child a piece of blank, unruled paper. Have him write the word in his natural script, without the capital letters, across the top of the paper. But have him write it TWICE AS BIG as he ordinarily would.

TWICE AS BIG, over and over and over again. Have him write it without looking at it. And never let him hesitate. Never let him stop in the middle. If he gets the word wrong, run through the first two steps with him again. And then go back to the TWICE AS BIG writing immediately.

Over and over again. Until he builds the writing of that word into a mechanically perfect skill. Until he gets that word down letter-perfect. Until he can write it correctly as casually as he writes his own signature.

Then it belongs to him. He has it—forever.

HOW TO MAKE THIS THREE-STEP SYSTEM WORK FOR YOUR CHILD EVERY DAY OF HIS SCHOOL CAREER

To learn a new word, as we have said before, means to know its meaning, its use in a sentence, its correct pronunciation, and its correct spelling. Until all these are letter-perfect, your child doesn't really own the word at all.

As your child advances through school, he will meet more and more important new words. Some of them he will misspell. Therefore he should have a Spelling Section in the back of his notebook.

Have him divide this Section into two parts. He should title the first part "Misspelled Words," and mark down in it any word he misspells.

Every night, have him take one of these misspelled words—no more—and use the system to teach himself its correct spelling.

Then, when he has that word letter-perfect, let him list it in the second part of the Spelling Section under the title "Mastered Words."

When he has listed about ten or twelve of these mastered words, dictate all of them to him in a short paragraph or story. Then check each of their spellings.

If any are misspelled, put them back in the first part of the Section, and start all over again. Because he hasn't established the correct habit yet.

But he will. Before you know it, you'll be amazed at the absolute precision he shows in these spelling tests.

And once he has mastered a word, encourage him to use it as often as possible. This will help him practice, to keep the correct spelling fresh in his mind. It will also build his confidence—show him over and over again that he no longer has the slightest reason to be afraid of misspelling that once-terrifying word.

In summary:

There's only one permissible grade in spelling; that is 100 per cent, letter-perfect.

This can be easily done if your child corrects every spelling error, individually, with this simple three-step method:

1. Detect the one or two letters in each difficult word that your child automatically spells wrong. Then CAPITALIZE the correct spelling of those letters till they stick out in front of your child's eyes like a sore thumb.

2. Think up *spell-alikes* for the hard letters that automatically remind your child of the correct way those hard letters should go.

3. And then give him the *feel* of his hand spelling the word right, over and over and over again, twice as big as life, till he jots it down correctly as easily and as automatically as he writes his own name.

This three-step system, applied daily to master one misspelled word, will make him a spelling whiz in far less time than you believed possible.

And now we turn to his ability to express his thoughts on paper—professional writing secrets that will enable him to turn in top-grade compositions almost as fast as the words can form in his mind.

CHAPTER 15

HOW YOUR CHILD CAN WRITE AS EASILY AND AS QUICKLY AS HE THINKS

In his school career alone, your child will be required to hand in at least four different kinds of written work: daily papers, research reports, themes, and examinations.

In addition, when he grows up, he will enter a world where he will be required to prepare his own résumés, inter-office memos, engineering reports, business and social letters, club minutes, and much more.

All of this vital work will be written. All of it will require that he be able to set down his thoughts, his suggestions, his goals on paper—so clearly and so persuasively that those papers serve as his best salesmen.

In his world, therefore, the ability to write well will be equally important to the ability to speak well. He must be as fluid with his pen as he is fluent with his tongue. He must be just as much at home writing a school theme as he is telling a friend about a ball game.

He must develop *ease in writing*.

Ease in writing, and precision in writing, come from two sources, both of which are available to your child:

1. *Practice*, and
2. *Planning*.

It is the combination of these two that constitute power writing. Let us see how you can build both of them into your child, starting with practice.

HOW TO MAKE WRITING EASY FOR YOUR CHILD, FROM THE VERY FIRST GRADE ON

Your child should practice writing as soon as he can spell out words on paper.

The fact that a six-year-old can read words in his primer, or that he can painfully spell each of them out on paper, really means very little. He is using those words only passively; they do not yet belong to him.

What you have to do is help him to put those words to *active use*, by showing him how to combine them into his own written sentences, and then link these sentences into stories.

This, among all your work with him, will be the most rewarding. All children love stories. They love to hear them. And, given the chance, they love to write them.

Why not start your child on such an imagination game of writing? Here's how easy it is:

Take your five-, or six-, or seven-year-old child, and give him a list of dramatic phrases. They can be any words that will spark his imagination. For example:

A broken bicycle. An old man. A crooked road. Two children.

From such phrases as these, let him weave his own story. It does not have to be long, of course, or perfect. Just a paragraph or two of sentences leading from one event to another.

It will take only a few minutes to write. It's fun. *And it will teach your child all these vital techniques*:

1. How to arrange his thoughts in order, so that one thought logically follows another.

2. How to divide each of those thoughts into a simple sentence, and then link those sentences up in to a story.

3. How to put those sentences down on paper both neatly and beautifully.

4. How to put the new words he has learned in school

into active use, so they become a co-ordinated part of his working vocabulary.

5. How to spell those words correctly, and get the feeling of writing them correctly on paper.

6. How to develop his imagination and creativity, so he can go from a few general hints to a fully developed tale.

Thus each one of these stories *puts together* the grammar and spelling and penmanship and word building your child has learned separately in his classes, *and makes them serve one dominant purpose—the expression of your child's own individual personality.*

WATCH HIS WRITING SKILL GROW

Give him one of these story assignments every week. If he makes mistakes, carefully and constructively point them out and have him rewrite them correctly.

Then, with every story he writes, read it aloud to the other members of the family; give him pride in the powers of his own self-expression. And, as always, be lavish with your praise.

As he grows older, start introducing stories about science, geography, history, and other subjects that he's becoming interested in in school. But always, in these stories, ask him for *his own* ideas, *his own* thoughts, *his own* stories, and not the content of any book.

These simple weekly exercises combined with the written work he's doing for school will develop a youngster—before you know it—who can write as easily and vividly as his teacher.

And now, to build precision and power into that writing, you teach him the equally simple technique of planning:

HOW HE CAN DISCOVER EXACTLY WHAT TO WRITE, FROM THE BEGINNING TO THE END OF THE THEME

Like reading, and perhaps even more so, writing demands a plan of attack, a definite goal that your child wants to achieve in every composition, and a definite plan to get there. A series of questions that puts him immediately on the right road, and keeps him there from the first word he writes to the last.

Let's look at such a series of direction-questions right now. Let's work out a typical theme, and see how these questions and their answers avoid errors, strengthen the power of what he has to say, and cut his writing time in half.

Let's take as our subject *Should America Try to Be First to Land a Man on the Moon?* This is a theme that your child might be asked to write in school any day. Let's assume that he answers the question with a "Yes," that America should try to land a man on the moon first, and see how he develops this subject.

First of all, he should ask himself these questions:

What exactly am I going to write about in this paper? (About whether America should try to be first to land a man on the moon.)

Can I express this key idea in a single sentence, before I begin to write? (Yes. America should be first to land a man on the moon.)

How much am I going to say about it? (I'm going to list the *reasons why* America should be first.)

What am I NOT going to say about it, because I don't have the room? (Two things: (1) I am not going to list any arguments for the other side, why America should *not* try to be first; and (2) I am not going to discuss any of the technical problems that we'll have to overcome to reach the moon.)

What specific points am I going to make about this idea? (The specific reasons why we should be first: Because it will help our prestige with the neutral nations. Because it will aid our economy. Because it will yield new inventions that we might otherwise not have discovered. Because it will give us new military strength. And because it fulfills man's destiny to explore the universe, in which America should always be in the forefront.)

How many of these points are there? (Five.)

In what order should they be arranged? Which should come first, second, third, and so on? (In this order: First, military strength; second, neutral nations; third, aid to the economy; fourth, scientific inventions; and fifth, exploration.

Which of these points are the most important; which should be given separate paragraphs? (All of them.)

Which points should I group into one paragraph? (None.)

What is the best way to catch my reader's interest? (Probably with a strong, emphatic assertion at the very beginning. Something like this: "There are at least five vital reasons why America should be first to put a man on the moon, any one of which would more than justify this project's cost.")

How do I end? Can I think of a good last sentence before I begin to write? (Yes. A summary sentence something like this: "Therefore, to keep our military strength from falling behind, to maintain our prestige with the uncommitted nations of the world, to strengthen our own economy, to receive the benefits from otherwise overlooked scientific discoveries, and to assure America's leadership at the forefront of human destiny, it is essential that this country be the first nation to place a man on the moon.")

HOW YOUR CHILD PERFECTS HIS COMPOSITION BEFORE HE BEGINS TO WRITE IT

The questions outlined above give your child two major benefits. They force him to choose a definite, easily handled topic, clearly formulated, concrete and specific, with no chance of wandering over its chosen limits. And they help him write about this topic one step at a time, with each step in its proper place.

Without such a blueprint, he simply won't know where he's going, and revising his paper will take him more time than originally writing it.

Now, once he has the answers to these questions, he arranges them quickly in a Main Thought Outline, just as he does in his daily reading. The process in both reading and writing is the same, but it is done in reverse. In writing, he gets his main thoughts first, builds them into an outline second, and then writes the paper itself on the basis of that outline.

Here is how he builds that outline.

He writes his title for the paper across the top of the outline: "*Why America Should Be First to Put a Man on the Moon.*"

He writes his first sentence directly below this title: "*There are at least five vital reasons why America should be the first to put a man on the moon, any one of which would more than justify this project's cost.*"

He takes his first major idea and marks it with the Roman numeral I:

"*I.   To keep our military strength from falling behind.*"

If this first major idea demands more than one paragraph to explain it fully, he then marks each one of these paragraphs with the capital letters A, B, C, and so on:

"*A.   To keep our missile strength from falling behind.*"

"*B.   To keep our missile-guidance strength from falling behind.*"

"*C.   To keep our military technology from falling behind.*"

Each of these paragraphs will have several sentences within it, to develop important details. These detail sentences are marked in the outline by Arabic numerals, and are placed under the capital letter paragraph to which they belong. For example, in paragraph A above, he would have these detail sentences:

"*A.   To keep our missile strength from falling behind.*"

1.   *Will force us to develop larger and larger rockets.*

2.   *More powerful engines.*

3. *Longer ranges.*
4. *And therefore heavier payloads.*

He continues on, developing every major idea in this way, marking them with the Roman numerals II, III, IV, and so on. Then breaking them into their separate paragraphs, and marking these with the capital letters A, B, C, and so on. Then outlining the individual detail-sentences with Arabic numerals 1, 2, 3, and so on, till he has finished outlining the entire paper.

He then writes in his concluding sentence, and he is finished with his outline. Here is a brief sample of what that outline will look like at that stage:

WHY AMERICA SHOULD BE FIRST TO PUT A MAN ON THE MOON

There are at least five vital reasons why America should be the first to put a man on the moon, any one of which would more than justify this project's cost:

I. To keep our military strength from falling behind.
  A. To keep our missile strength from falling behind.
    1. Will force us to develop larger and larger rockets.
    2. More powerful engines.
    3. Longer ranges.
    4. And therefore heavier payloads.
  B. To keep our missile-guidance strength from falling behind.
    1. Better radar.
    2. More sophisticated computers.
    3. Satellite tracking stations.
  C. To keep our military technology from falling behind.
    1. Research facilities.
    2. Manufacturing plants.
    3. Testing and feedback.
    4. Space education.

II.   To maintain our prestige with the uncommitted nations of the world.

      A.   To prevent a Russian "reign of terror."

And so on, till the outline is finished.

HOW TO WRITE THE FINISHED DRAFT OF THE PAPER

From this point on, the final draft of the composition writes itself.

Your child takes the title and the first sentence and puts them down on the paper. He then takes main idea I and phrases it into his next paragraph, like this:

"First of all, of course, such a project is necessary to keep our military strength from falling behind that of the Soviet Union."

Now he takes each of the three paragraphs under this main idea I, and builds them according to the outline, like this:

"In our comparative missile strength alone, the moon project will yield vast benefits. It will force us to develop larger rockets. It will force us to devise larger engines to propel them. These larger engines will give us longer ranges for all our missiles, space and military. And they will result in heavier payloads, wherever we have to deliver them.

"The same exact benefits will be felt in our missile-guidance program. From moon project research, we will gain better radar. We will develop more sophisticated computer systems, with faster speeds and greater accuracy. And we may even find ourselves with a network of satellite tracking stations spread across the globe."

And so on. Paragraph by paragraph, right through the entire paper.

When he is through, your child will have a composition that develops his subject thoroughly, that presents his points in logical, persuasive order, that makes good reading and makes sense, and that earns top grades.

TIPS ON WRITING THAT DE-
VELOP CLARITY AND POWER

1.   Every paragraph should contain only *one* main idea and the details that develop it. When your child goes on to discuss a second main idea, he should start a new paragraph.

This has been shown over and over again in the examples we have given above.

2.   Each sentence, in its turn, should contain only *one* idea. The great mistake most students make is in trying to crowd too many ideas into a single sentence. This results in huge, clumsy, poorly graded sentences. When you get to a second idea—or when you find two or more ideas crowded against each other in a single sentence—separate them and build each into its own sentence.

EXAMPLE:

WRONG WAY: *After we arrived home from the trip, tired and dirty, we immediately went upstairs, where we unpacked our clothes and hung them up, before we allowed ourselves to take a shower and go to bed.*

CLEARER AND MORE POWERFUL: *We arrived home from the trip, tired and dirty. We immediately went upstairs. Yet, before we allowed ourselves to take a shower and go to bed, we unpacked our clothes and hung them up.*

3.   Long sentences in school compositions are usually confused sentences. One sure way to avoid this mistake, and to write clearer, stronger sentences, is to keep the subject and predicate of each sentence as close together as possible.

EXAMPLE:

WRONG WAY: *The man whom Tom had seen earlier that day running away from the bank spun around when he saw Tom.*

The subject of this sentence is "man" and its predicate is "spun." The reason the sentence is confusing is that this subject and predicate are separated so widely by the clause "whom Tom had seen earlier that day running away from the bank." Therefore, to make these two thoughts far more powerful and clear, they should be separated like this:

RIGHT WAY: *It was the man whom Tom had seen earlier that day running away from the bank. When he saw Tom again, he spun around.*

4.   Make sure your child's sentences are connected correctly. He has to point out the relation between one sentence and the next. Otherwise, his reader won't know where his train of thought is going.

Connecting words are *and, yet, but, so, or, for, however, therefore, thus, otherwise, because, from, such, this,* and so on. They point out to your child's reader what his second sentence has to do with his first, what his third has to do with his second, and so on.

EXAMPLES: A good exercise for your child would be to go through a few pages of any good book and underline the connecting words the author uses. Have him bring the book to you when he has underlined a page or two in this way. Ask him to tell you exactly how each connecting word ties in one sentence with the sentence that goes before.

This way, he will develop skill in using these tie-in words, and his papers will be a powerful procession of closely woven thoughts.

In summary:

The ability to write well is as important as the ability to speak well, and it is as easy to learn.

Ease in writing comes from two sources: practice and planning.

In regard to practice, your child should start to write his own compositions as soon as he can spell words on paper. He should write one a week for you, from the first grade on.

He should also be taught, from the very beginning, the principles of planning. Before he starts to write a word, he should already have defined his subject, his main thoughts, and his opening and closing sentences.

And he should have arranged them in paragraph-by-paragraph order in a Main Thought Outline, so his paper will practically write itself when he sits down to begin it.

PART FOUR

MATHEMATICS CAN BE FUN, IF YOU DO IT THIS WAY

CHAPTER 16

HOW ANY PARENT CAN HELP HIS CHILD WITH MATHEMATICS, EVEN IF HE CAN'T ADD TWO AND TWO

Unfortunately, most parents, like their children, are awed by mathematics. They realize that it produces more school failures than any other subject. They have unpleasant memories of it from their own classroom days. They believe that it consists of nothing more than brain-twisting problems, with no relation to everyday life, done for the amusement of super-eggheads in ivory towers.

Nothing, of course, could be further from the truth.

When you get right down to it, the basic principle of all mathematics, from arithmetic to calculus, is as simple as ABC, and as practical as a screw driver. It can be stated in one clear sentence:

Mathematics is THINKING BY STEPS to solve problems.

Just that, and nothing more. Mathematics is the art of solving problems, STEP BY STEP. The key is STEP BY STEP.

Even the most complicated problems can be broken down into one simple step following another. Once you teach your child this secret, you have shown him how to lick mathematics.

HOW STEP-BY-STEP WORKS

Let's take a closer look at this basic principle.

Mathematics is simply *a way of arriving at correct answers* when you are given a certain set of facts called a problem. It is *thinking by steps* to get from what is given to

161

what is asked for. It is the art of solving a problem, *one easy step at a time*, to reach the correct conclusion.

Approached in this way, mathematics becomes not only simple, but fun. More fun than solving crossword puzzles or riddles, but developed step by step in exactly the same way.

It is within the reach of every child—and every parent. *For even if the technical problems themselves may be beyond you, the simple method of arriving at their correct answers is easily within your supervision and control.*

WHAT THIS SECTION WILL DO FOR YOUR CHILD

Any parent, even if he cannot add two and two, can help his child in three vital, *nontechnical* areas of mathematics, where 90 per cent of a good start lies. These three areas are:

1. Preventing careless mistakes, which robs most children of 20 per cent of their mathematics grades every day. Chapter 15 will show you how to cut out this waste 20 per cent overnight.

2. Making abstract parts of problems as real to your child as his own thumb. Chapter 16 will show you how to do this with a few quick lines of your pencil.

3. Unraveling complicated word problems and preceding step by step to the correct answer. Chapter 17 will show you how to make even the longest, most involved problem nothing more than a series of easy steps, that your child can do in one-two-three order.

But first, right now, let's take a look at some:

BASIC HINTS FOR TOP GRADES IN MATHEMATICS

1. No matter how bright your child, there are certain fundamentals that must be memorized so thoroughly that instant correct results are given back to you every time. For example, the addition and multiplication tables.

Here, there is no substitution for *drill*. No substitution

for *practice,* over and over again, in cars, at the dinner table, before he goes to bed, and when he is brushing his hair every morning.

Over and over again. To himself, in his classroom, to you. The right answers must become so much a second nature that there is no counting, no picking or scratching with a pencil, no moving of fingers or lips till he tells you the right answer.

2. As he builds up this mastery of fundamentals, and as his recitations give you the feel of his mathematical strengths and weaknesses, you will notice that certain numbers give him more trouble than others. For example, number 9 is a trouble-maker for most children in addition, subtraction, and multiplication. But your own child may have his own particular bogeyman—6 or 5 or 7.

In any case, watch for that trouble-maker. Identify it as soon as possible. Then give it special drills to eliminate it. Keep pounding at it, over and over again, till it becomes as automatic as all the rest.

3. In any kind of mathematics, from the most simple addition to the most complex calculus, *each new step builds directly on the step that came before it.*

For example, your child must learn to add one and one before he can add two and two.

He must master his addition table before he can learn to multiply.

He must master his multiplication table before he can learn to divide.

And he must be completely in control—foolproof and mistake-proof—in addition, subtraction, multiplication, and division—before he can even begin to think of learning algebra or any other branch of higher mathematics.

Each step builds on the step that came directly before it. Therefore your child must completely master that first step before he can go on to the second.

He must understand each of those steps—each of them

in turn—so completely that it becomes second nature to him. And only then can he go on to the next.

To do this, he must again *practice*. Do sample problems for each new step. Go over and over them. Eliminate any possibility of confusion or mistake. Never let him leave any classroom with any problem or process unclear in his mind. Have him question and requestion his teacher till he understands it completely.

Again—*practice*. The same day-after-day practice he devotes to mastering football or tennis or golf. For every new step he learns in any course in mathematics, he must practice.

Then and only then will the next step in the course be as easy as the one he has just finished. Only then will he be able to zip right through those math courses, without constantly being lost and bewildered, constantly being forced to backtrack and learn again something he should have mastered the first time.

4. Because one step depends so completely on the step that went before it, your child has to pay special care to his mathematics notebook. It must contain:

a. A basic vocabulary of every new term he has learned in the course. That term must be listed alphabetically, defined in a sentence, and illustrated with a sample problem and solution showing how it applies to the problems he'll be given in his tests.

b. A listing of every single new operation he has learned in the course (for example, how to add fractions that total less than one; how to add fractions that total more than one; how to add whole numbers and fractions together, and so on). Each new operation should be named, and accompanied by a sample problem and solution showing each step in the solution broken down in the exact correct order.

c. A mistake page listing every error that he has made in previous exams and the correct method of solving it. For a thorough discussion of this all-important point, see Chapter 19.

5. And because of this dependence of one step upon the step that came before it, sickness or accident that causes your child to be absent from class is a far greater problem in mathematics than in any other subject.

In mathematics, your child must make up the steps he missed when he was sick, before he can ever begin to understand the work his class is doing upon his return. You have to get him to understand that lost material—immediately, so he doesn't fall further behind.

This means night work. If you can, teach it to him yourself. If you can't, see if his teacher will give him after-class help. If she can't do this, then get a tutor at once.

Again, *drill* him. Pump that missing information into him, and test, test, test. You'll know he has caught up when his daily classroom papers come back to their previous standard. And don't settle for anything less.

In summary:

Mathematics can be made easy for your child once he does it the right way.

The vital secret he must learn is to do his mathematics problems *step by step*. And to master one step before he goes on to the next.

He does this by learning three simple techniques:

1. Neatness and precision, to make sure he gets every step down right, without a single unnecessary mistake.

2. Translating abstract steps into concrete terms that he can easily understand.

3. Unraveling complicated word problems so he can automatically do them, one simple step at a time.

Let's now examine these techniques, one by one.

CHAPTER 17

It is a proved fact that careless mistakes, sloppy copying, slips of the pen, and just plain inattention account for approximately 20 per cent of all errors in mathematics.

Think of this fact for one moment. If your child is now bringing home, say, a 70 on his math papers, simply substituting precision for sloppiness in his work could improve that grade—overnight—20 per cent, or 14 points, or bring his work up to an 84.

One simple demand on your part—for neatness, accuracy, precision—will make that much difference. *Isn't it worth a few minutes of your time, right now, to teach him these three fundamental rules that can give him one-fifth better grades overnight?*

PRECISION RULE NUMBER ONE: WRITE EACH NUMBER CORRECTLY.

Most children scrawl their numbers, rather than write them: 4's look like 9's, or 7's; 2's are mistaken for 3's. Error is built into his work at the very beginning, and he never has a chance to overcome it.

Your first task, therefore, in building precision into your child's mathematics is to check each one of the ten numbers he writes down on paper. Every one of those numbers must stand out sharp and clear, without the slightest chance of a mistake, even to a casual glance.

Here are the most common errors children make in writing numbers, and the correct way each numeral should look:

1　　2　　3　　4　　5　　6　　7　　8　　9　　0

1　2　3　4　5　6　7　8　9　0

Make every number as precise as it is on the printed page, and your child has taken a giant step to better math grades in a few short minutes.

PRECISION RULE NUMBER TWO: PLACE COLUMNS OF FIGURES EXACTLY UNDER ONE ANOTHER.

The second great careless error that robs your child of top math grades is a zigzag column. A single number allowed to wander out of position is a sure guarantee that the problem is going to be done wrong.

Make sure your child places all numbers in precisely the right position in every problem. The columns of figures should form straight vertical lines—with the 1's precisely under the 1, the 10's precisely under the 10's, the 100's precisely under the 100's, and so on.

There is a simple way of checking to see whether your child is doing this right. Take a ruler and draw lines between the columns of figures. If the lines do not touch a single numeral, the columns are correct. If they do, then have him recopy the problems again until he gets them right.

Here is a typical sloppy column in addition, and the same problem written correctly. You can see the difference at a glance.

$$
\begin{array}{rr}
1\$54.72 & 7.\ \$54.72 \\
3.02 & 3.02 \\
105.07 & 103.07 \\
70.27 & 70.27 \\
259.30 & 259.36 \\
47.00 & 47.00 \\
\hline
161.73 & 161.73
\end{array}
$$

PRECISION RULE NUMBER THREE: COPY EACH PROBLEM CORRECTLY.

No child can get an answer right unless he first has the problem right. He first has to get it out of his book, or off the class blackboard, and on to his paper precisely correct. A single figure miscopied can send him into a tailspin of confusion for a full hour, while he tries to find out where he went wrong.

Therefore your child must learn the vital technique of copying correctly. Here's how it goes:

1. He copies word for word, number for number. He leaves nothing out, condenses nothing, abbreviates nothing. Every mark that is on the board should be on his paper, in exactly the same position.

2. When he has finished copying the problem, he checks each line, and then the problem as a whole, in this way. First, he counts the number of lines in the problem on the board; then he counts the lines on his paper to see that they match. Then he checks the contents of each line, one by one, to make sure each figure matches. Only then does he begin to work.

3. On word problems he underlines each of the key

words in the problem on his paper (see Chapter 18 for a description of *key words* in mathematics). Then he checks each key word with the board to make sure he has them all, and they are all correct. Only then does he begin to work.

4. At the end of his solution, if the answer does not seem logical, he checks the problem against the board once again. He may spot a figure miscopied now that he had overlooked before. And this may save him precious moments of wrestling to correct a wrong answer whose error had lain in the very beginning.

In summary:

Approximately 20 per cent of all errors in mathematics are made from pure inaccuracy.

Without absolute precision in every step he makes in mathematics, your child is beaten before his mind even begins to work.

He gains this vital precision by learning three simple techniques:

1. To make sharp, clear numbers that can't be mistaken even at a quick glance.

2. By making ruler-straight columns, with each number precisely in the right place.

3. By copying his problems exactly—photographically—with every number exactly as it is given to him.

Once he has made this habit of precision second nature, he is then ready to learn how to make abstract problems as plain and as simple as his own thumb. We now turn to this technique.

CHAPTER 18

HOW TO MAKE ABSTRACT IDEAS CONCRETE
FOR YOUR CHILD

One of the most difficult parts of mathematics for most children is the fact that it is abstract, that it deals with ideas that he cannot see or touch or picture easily in his mind's eye.

Therefore these abstract ideas become hard for him to work with, *when they would really be quite easy if someone just made them into physical models for him to see.*

Most parents instinctively recognize this fact. When you taught your child how to count, for example, you did not ask him to try to add the abstract number "one" with another abstract number "one" to get the abstract number "two."

Instead, you gave him *physical objects* to add—one *ball* with another *ball* to make two *balls,* or one *marble* with another *marble* to make two *marbles.* Only later did he learn to separate the numbers from the objects and add one and one of *anything.*

The same rule—the same construction of physical models —holds true throughout his entire school career. From time to time, your child is going to be introduced to new abstract ideas. He is not going to be able to see or touch or picture them immediately. And he is going to have trouble with them for this reason alone.

Therefore your job is to give him physical models that make these ideas easy to work with.

Let's look at some of the most common of these abstract ideas. Let's see how easy it is to turn them into pictures or models that your child can see and move around, once he's given the key.

Let's start with one of the hardest ideas to picture in grade school, one that causes most people most trouble throughout their entire lives.

HOW TO MAKE FRACTION MODELS.

A *fraction* is a part of a whole. This is its word definition, but it is extremely hard to picture. So let's work with fractions, not only with words and numbers, but with pictures. The fraction ¼ looks like this:

The complete box represents a whole, or the number 1. The fraction ¼ is one-fourth of that whole box. Your child should learn to shade the fraction (in this case, the ¼), to make it stand out from the remainder of the whole.

You may also draw a picture of ¼ without representing the whole box that it is a part of. You do it in this way:

Now, once you learn the idea of making these fraction pictures, working with fractions becomes as simple as adding or subtracting building blocks. Let's take a few examples:

TO ADD FRACTIONS THE PICTURE WAY.

Suppose your child is given the problem: **Add ¼ + ¼ + ¼.**

He immediately draws this picture:

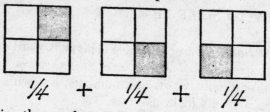

Notice that each ¼ is shaded in a different part of the whole box. This makes adding easier in the final answer.

Of course the answer is now perfectly evident, even at a glance. It is:

It is as easy as counting blocks. And it remains that easy, even when your child goes on to more complicated problems that might otherwise have given him weeks of trouble. Like this:

TO REDUCE IMPROPER FRACTIONS THE PICTURE WAY.

An *improper fraction* is a fraction that adds up to more than one, and should therefore be changed to a whole number and a proper fraction. For example, your child may be given this problem:

Change the improper fraction ⁹⁄₄ to a mixed number. (A mixed number is a whole number and a proper fraction, in this case 2¼.)

To do the problem, your child first lays out the 9 fourths, like this:

Then he simply groups them into wholes, as easily as assembling blocks, like this:

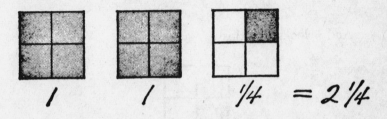

The answer is as plain as the nose on his face—2¼. Simply a matter of grouping and counting physical units that he can see and touch.

Of course, he uses these physical models only until he understands fractions so well that they become second nature to him. Then he automatically drops the models—just as he dropped the balls and marbles of his first countings—and uses the now-mastered abstract idea of fractions to go on with.

One more example will make this clear.

TO ADD AND SUBTRACT FRACTIONS WITH DIFFERENT DENOMINATORS THE PICTURE WAY.

A *denominator* is the part of the fraction that is under the line (the /4 in ¼, the /2 in ½, and so on). To add or subtract fractions with different denominators, your child may be given a problem like this:

If Susie needs ½ yard of cloth for a doll's dress, and ¼ yard for the jacket, how much cloth does she need in all?

Your child can easily solve this by remembering that ½ looks like this:

And ¼ looks like this:

So added together, they form this picture:

Thus different denominators become as easy to work with as problems having the same denominators.

But as your child grows more at home with fractions, he can forget about drawing pictures for each problem, and go on to the faster way of working with the different fractions themselves.

To help him do this—to help him picture the relation of many different denominators at once—you give him a new model. This time it is a Denominator Chart, like this:

1							
½				½			
¼		¼		¼		¼	
⅛	⅛	⅛	⅛	⅛	⅛	⅛	⅛
¹⁄₁₆ ¹⁄₁₆	¹⁄₁₆ ¹⁄₁₆	¹⁄₁₆ ¹⁄₁₆	¹⁄₁₆ ¹⁄₁₆	¹⁄₁₆ ¹⁄₁₆	¹⁄₁₆ ¹⁄₁₆	¹⁄₁₆ ¹⁄₁₆	¹⁄₁₆ ¹⁄₁₆

Notice that you are still working with pictures, but that this picture is more abstract than the blocks you were building for him before. Thus you are moving him step by step to mastery of the truly abstract principles of mathematics, but giving him complete understanding and self-confidence every step of the way.

OTHER MATHEMATICAL MODELS YOU MAY BUILD FOR YOUR CHILD

Decimals are hard for most children only because they don't realize that they've been working with them all their lives, in the form of dollars and pennies.

A penny is a decimal part of a dollar (one-hundredth). So is a dime (one-tenth, or $.10). So is a quarter (one-fourth, or $.25). So is a half dollar (one-half, or $.50).

Train your child, at least at the beginning, to substitute the word *pennies*, for *decimal points* when he begins *to* solve decimal problems.

Thus the problem "What part is .25 of one?" becomes "What part is 25 cents of one dollar?", which becomes "How many quarters in a dollar?", which he can answer instantly.

All other decimal problems are equally a cinch, once your child thinks of them in terms of money.

Percentages are just multiplying by pennies. A percentage point is nothing more than a decimal point with the period in front of it removed and the per-cent symbol (%) placed after it. Thus 10% is equal to .10. And your child already knows that .10 equals $.10 or 10¢.

Thus 10% = .10 = $.10 = 10¢.

Percentages are used to multiply other numbers by. If you want to find 25% of 100, you multiply 100 by 25%, or .25, or have a "bankruptcy sale" where you're only going to get 25¢ on the dollar. Thus 25% of 100 is 25.

This image of a "bankruptcy sale" makes percentages quite easy to do, for the simple reason that it turns the abstract idea of "percentages" into physical dollars and cents. Try it for a while with your child. The results may amaze you.

Algebra may be thought of as a game, a series of riddles in which someone hides a number and your child has to find it.

The number that's hidden is replaced by a letter of the alphabet. For example, $x = 2 + 3$. To find x, your child simply adds 2 + 3.

The puzzles get harder as the game goes along, but the rules are still the same. Letters are substituted for numbers, and your child has to rearrange them, step by step, to find the numbers.

Thought of in this way, algebra becomes quite simple, and quite a lot of fun.

Geometry was invented to solve physical problems— engineering problems, building problems, farm problems. Later, it lost this solid nature and became quite abstract. Your job it to make it physical again. You do this by building, or helping your child build, models. Triangles made of matchsticks. Circles made of string. Rubber balls serving as spheres. Physical objects that your child can measure, open and close, compare one with the other.

This is especially important in solid geometry, where it is practically impossible for him to understand the course without physical models. Here, five minutes spent taking apart and putting together a plastic model of, say, a cylinder, will be worth two hours of abstract book study.

In summary:

Some of the most important ideas in mathematics are abstract—extremely difficult for your child to see or touch or picture in his mind clearly.

Because they are abstract, these ideas are hard for your child to work with until somebody makes them solid and real for him.

This is done by building physical models of those ideas for him. This chapter has listed several physical models that you can easily give him.

These models help him grasp the fundamental idea easily and quickly. Later on, when it has become second nature to him, he will no longer need the model, and will be able to work directly with the abstract idea itself.

Now we show him how to apply almost the same technique to break down complicated problems into a series of simple, easy-to-do steps.

CHAPTER 19

HOW TO MAKE COMPLICATED PROBLEMS
HALF-SOLVE THEMSELVES

In the first four years of his school career, your child will concentrate on the fundamental skills of addition, subtraction, multiplication, and division.

Starting with the fifth grade, however, and continuing past college and throughout his adult life, if he pursues a business or engineering or scientific career, he will be presented with far more complicated problems.

Problems that involve as many as a dozen or two dozen individual steps.

Problems that are given to him out of order, and must be rearranged before he can even begin to solve them.

Problems that are stated in words as well as numbers, and demand that he can read as well as figure.

These complicated word-and-number problems *cannot*, of course, be solved by blindly rushing into them. Like any other part of your child's studies, technique is demanded in order to simplify and organize them.

Not one, but three separate skills are required in order to master them:

    1. Reading.
    2. Reorganizing.
    3. Problem solving.

Let's examine these techniques, one by one:

WHY ARE WORD PROBLEMS SO HARD FOR YOUR CHILD? FOR THESE REASONS:

First, because they involve several steps. They are actually several little problems wrapped up in one.

Second, because they demand reading skill as well as figuring skill. Your child must understand every word of the vocabulary he is reading. And he must be able to pick out the key parts of the problem by using that vocabulary.

Third, these parts of the problem are often not presented in the order that must be followed to solve them. Thus, after they are first read and understood, their order must be reversed so that each part of the problem can be solved in its proper turn.

Fourth, often there is a "hidden problem" that makes up one of the parts, which is never even stated at all. This "hidden problem" must thus be identified, stated by your child, and then solved—all in its proper place.

And finally, since all these sub-problems are stated in words, there are no plus or minus signs to tell him what operations to perform. Where in number problems the correct operations are given to him by the signs, here he must furnish them himself.

HOW TO OVERCOME ALL OF THESE OBSTACLES BY THIS ONE SIMPLE TECHNIQUE

Because of all these complications, procedure—step-by-step attack—is vital for word problems. Choice of method is crucial. The wrong procedure not only has a fifty-fifty chance of coming out wrong, but it will probably take your child five to ten times as long as the right method.

For example, take this typical grade-school problem:

If apples are sold at *two for five cents, how many* can be bought for *eighty-five cents?*

STEP ONE. READ THE PROBLEM.

The first thing your child does, of course, is *actively* read the entire problem, word by word, slowly and carefully, with pencil in hand.

All the skills he has learned in reading come into play here. For unless he reads the problem correctly, and understands it completely, nothing else he does can give him a right answer.

In fact, a leading educator at Columbia University has said this: "In advanced math, precise reading is actually 90 per cent of the battle."

Therefore, your child *double-reads* the problem. He reads it the first time to get its over-all meaning. And then he reads it again to underline the key words.

When he has finished underlining it, the problem looks like this:

If apples are sold at *two for five cents, how many* can be bought for *eighty-five cents?*

STEP TWO: ASK, "WHAT IS GIVEN?"

Now, when he has understood the problem completely and marked the key facts, he asks himself: "What is given? What does this problem tell me? What are the facts I have to start with?"

In this case, they are simply that apples are sold at *two for five cents.*

STEP THREE: ASK, "WHAT ANSWER IS CALLED FOR?"

In this case, "*How many* apples will *eighty-five cents* buy?"

STEP FOUR: ASK, "IS THERE A HIDDEN QUESTION IN THIS PROBLEM?" IF SO, WHAT IS IT?

In this case, the answer is yes, there is a hidden question. It is, "How many times does five cents go into eighty-five cents?"

STEP FIVE: ASK, "HOW MANY STEPS DO I NEED TO SOLVE THIS PROBLEM?"

Now your child decides how many little problems there are in this big problem.

In this case, there are two:

1. Finding out how many nickels there are in eighty-five cents.

2. Finding out how many apples this number of nickels gives when every nickel brings two apples.

STEP SIX: FIND OUT WHETHER TO ADD, SUBTRACT, MULTIPLY, OR DIVIDE IN EACH STEP.

In Step 1, he must divide 5 cents into 85 cents to get the number of nickels.

In Step 2, he must multiply the answer from Step 1 by two apples to get his final answer.

STEP SEVEN: MAKE SURE THE STEPS ARE IN THE RIGHT ORDER.

He must ask himself, "What do I need to do first? What do I need to do second?" And so on. Then, if necessary, he must rewrite the problem in the correct order to solve it.

In this case, the steps are already in the correct order.

STEP EIGHT: DO EACH STEP IN TURN.

In this case:

$$1)\ 5\overline{)85} = 17$$
$$\phantom{1)\ 5\overline{)8}}\frac{5}{35}$$

$$2)\ 17 \times 2 = \underline{\underline{34}}\ apples\ for\ 85\cancel{c}$$

He must, of course, remember to use the answer found in Step 1 as one of his figures in Step 2.

And when he finds the final answer, he should not only write it down but underline it.

STEP NINE: CHECK THE ANSWER TO MAKE SURE IT'S RIGHT.

He does this by reversing the two steps, like this:

To check Step 2:

$$2\overline{)34} \begin{array}{c} 17 \\ \underline{2} \\ 14 \\ 14 \end{array} = 17$$

To check Step 1:

$$\begin{array}{r} 17 \\ \times 5 \\ \hline 85 \end{array} = 85$$

He now has his right answer, and he knows that answer is right. Make sure he follows this simple procedure for every word problem he encounters, and you'll be amazed at how easy they all become.

HOW TO TURN "HOPELESS PROBLEMS" INTO SNAPS.

Word problems are one of the two great bogeymen of advanced mathematics. The other terror of the classroom is the long, complicated problem involving half a dozen to a dozen steps.

Most children freeze up when given an involved problem that doesn't resolve itself into a simple, easy answer, or that takes a long series of steps.

But these problems are just as easy as $2 + 2 = 4$, if your child only *works them out one step at a time,* and writes down each of the answers.

The secret is simple: *hard, complicated problems are just a lot of easy problems strung together.*

Therefore the trick in getting your child high grades in his higher math courses is simply this:

Make him see that these problems are a series of simple, easy steps.

Make him do these problems one step after another, each in its proper order, and each written down on his paper.

The procedure is simple. The problem is broken down into a series of steps. Each step is taken in turn, and written down on the work paper. No step, no matter how simple, may be omitted. No step may be done in your child's head, or placed on another sheet of paper.

Each step is written out, solved, and the solution used to help solve the next step in its turn.

This way, your child eliminates the three major nontechnical sources of error throughout his entire use of higher mathematics.

1. He doesn't take crazy short cuts that can trip him up in a dozen different ways.

2. He doesn't strive for quick, done-in-the-head answers that aren't thought through.

3. *He concentrates on the PROCEDURE by which he gets the answer,* and not on the answer itself, which comes automatically out of that procedure.

IN MATHEMATICS, *METHOD* IS THE KEY TO SUCCESS.

In mathematics, strange as it may seem at first glance,

the correct answers are not nearly as important as the way your child arrives at them.

The means—the methods—the procedures your child learns in his math classes are the real treasures he carries away with him into later life. Individual problems and answers come and go. But the correct procedures will continue to give him thousands of correct answers, all the rest of his life.

Therefore remind him over and over again that the great value of a correct answer is that it shows him that he knows how to use the correct procedure.

Emphasize mastery of method. This leads his mind away from fruitless copying of correct answers. It focuses his attention on getting the procedure right today, so that it can automatically give him the correct answer every time.

WHAT TO DO IF A PROBLEM HAS YOUR CHILD STOPPED COLD

One last hint. Every child, no matter how bright, runs into a problem from time to time that just stumps him. In this case, there is a simple procedure that may break that roadblock immediately. Here it is:

1. Have him read it again from the very start. He should look especially for clues that he may have missed before. It may even be helpful to have him rewrite the problem again on a fresh sheet of paper.

2. Go over his steps. A simple error in addition may have thrown him off.

3. Try substituting simpler numbers for those given in the problem. If it is a problem in algebra, try restating it in arithmetical numbers. This may make it simple enough that he can see the correct procedures he should follow at a glance.

4. Have him go on to the next problem for a moment. This may supply the needed mental connection.

5. Let him leave the problem for the night. Then perhaps he can solve it the next morning when his mind is fresh, and he's had a chance to absorb the procedure.

6. Look up a similar problem or procedure in another book. Perhaps a new author's way of explaining the problem will make it clear to your child.

7. If nothing else works, be sure he discusses the problem with his teacher the next day. Check back with him that night to make certain he now understands it completely. Follow the Golden Error procedure outlined in the next chapter.

In summary:

Complicated math problems are made simple in these two ways:

If it is a word problem, by following this nine-step procedure:

1. Read the problem.
2. Ask what is given.
3. Ask what answer is called for.
4. Ask if there is a hidden question in the problem. If so, what it is.
5. Ask how many steps are needed to solve the problem.
6. Find out what operation must be done in each step.
7. Make sure the steps are in the right order.
8. Do each step in turn.
9. Check the answer to make sure it's right.

If it is not a word problem, but is a long, complicated problem with many steps, by following this procedure:

Break each problem down into a series of steps.

Do each step in turn.

Write every part of every step down on the work paper, omitting nothing.

Use the answer from one part to help get the correct answer from the next.

And so on until the problem is finished and right.

PART FIVE

MASTERING FACTS—

THE ART OF REMEMBERING AND REVIEW

CHAPTER 20

ERRORS—THE ROYAL ROAD TO KNOWLEDGE

Every student, no matter how bright or slow he is, learns some facts quickly and has trouble with others.

Those he learns easily require little outside help. It is the troublesome fact, the error-causing fact, the fact that blocks the road to understanding that we must concentrate upon with him.

The telltale symptom of trouble, of course, is a mistake in his work. Most parents are troubled by these mistakes. *They do not realize that if they are handled correctly, they are worth their weight in gold.*

Why? Because a mistake is actually nothing more or less than a signpost in your child's work that identifies misunderstanding.

And by analyzing what went wrong in each of those mistakes, and correcting it, you will help him achieve a far deeper level of understanding and competence than he could ever gain without them.

This is perfectly in accord with the prime rule of all self-improvement—*work on weaknesses.* His strengths he will always have. But his weaknesses must be identified and gone over and over again until they are no longer there.

Let us therefore examine this technique of turning a mistake into gold. It is as simple as this:

HOW YOUR CHILD CAN PROFIT FROM HIS MISTAKES.

It is never enough for your child simply to glance at his daily paper when it is handed back to him, and notice that he has made an error on it.

189

Every day, on every error he makes, he must be able to answer these three questions about that error before he is allowed to go on to his new work:

1.   Where in the problem did he make the mistake?

2.   What did he do wrong that caused him to make that mistake?

3.   What is the correct operation that will avoid that same kind of mistake in the future?

Let's see how these three questions turn errors into accomplishments.

STEP ONE: LOCATE THE ERROR.

For example, let's say that he came home with a wrong answer in a long-division problem.

He knows that the answer is wrong, but *where exactly* did it go wrong?

Was it a mistake in multiplication or subtraction inside the problem?

Was it only one mistake or several?

Have him break the problem down into steps. Check each step to find out which one went wrong. Don't rest till he can pinpoint the exact step where each error occurred.

STEP TWO: FIND OUT WHAT CAUSED IT.

Now, when he's located the exact spot where the error occurred, he has to identify its cause.

Let's say that it was a mistake in one of his multiplications. He multiplied 6 by 9 and came up with 52.

What caused him to make this mistake?

Was it simply carelessness? Or is that mistake a warning to the two of you that he's weak in multiplying 9's?

STEP THREE: CORRECT THE CAUSE OF THE ERROR.

If it was carelessness, review with him again the techniques of checking an answer to make sure it's right before he hands it in. And review the Neatness and Precision chapter given in the section before.

If, however, he does show a weakness in 9's, stop everything and review the 9 section of the multiplication table with him. Do it over and over again until it becomes automatic with him, and automatically right.

Remember, you have to correct the *cause* of an error before you can permanently correct the error itself. If you do not correct the cause first, the error will simply repeat itself later on.

STEP FOUR: CORRECT THE ERROR ITSELF.

Now take a fresh sheet of paper, copy the problem onto that paper yourself, and have him work it again.

This time it should come out right. If it does, file it away and come back to it the following week. Give it to him again on a fresh piece of paper.

If he gets it right again, enter it into his Mistakes Made page at the back of his notebook.

STEP FIVE: HAVE HIM DO SIMILAR PROBLEMS TO MAKE SURE HE'S GOT THE CORRECT TECHNIQUE.

At the same time, give him several other problems with 9's in them. Concentrate on those 9's. Within a short time he'll have mastered them all, and the correct answers will flow from his pen, with perfect confidence.

In summary:

Follow this same technique with every step he makes.
Break the problem down into steps.
See which step went wrong.
Find out why.
Correct the cause of the error.
Have him rework the problem the right way.

And keep him doing it over and over again until the right answer is absolutely automatic.

This way mistakes help him rather than harm him. You are helping him climb from mere "good student" to champion. Because he won't make that mistake—or its first cousin—again. Because you have helped him remove a misunderstanding-roadblock from his mind.

This process of turning errors into achievements is one of the finest forms of review. We now turn to a complete discussion of this all-important subject.

CHAPTER 20

HOW YOUR CHILD CAN BURN FACTS, LESSONS,
WHOLE SUBJECTS INTO HIS MIND—FOR GOOD

We are now ready to review what your child has learned so far in this book, and tie it together into one over-all plan for mastering any subject he is given in school.

Mastering a course—any course—consists of the following logical steps:

1. Your child finds out what it is that he has to learn in each assignment in the course.

2. He reads that assignment to get at the heart of its meaning.

3. He writes that core meaning down in his notebook in a few brief sentences or phrases, related to each other through the outline form.

4. He ties the outline of that assignment into the assignment that came before it.

5. *He then reviews as much as he has studied of the entire book or course EVERY WEEK, to get an over-all view of everything he has studied.*

6. *At the end of the term, a week or two before the final test, he then makes a final review of his strengths and weaknesses throughout the entire course. Here he finds out what he knows well; what he should know better; what he really does not know at all.*

And on the basis of this final review, he creates the final study schedule for the week before the test.

This, then, is your child's Plan of Mastery for his school subjects. We have already discussed Steps 1 through 4. We now turn to Steps 5 and 6—the strategy of review, of fixing the heart of his course permanently in his mind.

WHAT REVIEW IS *NOT*

First of all, let us define review by saying quite definitely what it is *not*.

Review is *not* cramming, *not* last-minute effort, *not* the desperate piling up of information in frenzied disorder.

This type of cramming always fails. It always has failed. It always will fail.

Why? Because it attempts to store up large quantities of *unorganized* material. And without organization, there can be no memory. Material crammed into your child's brain leaks out again as fast as it goes in.

WHAT IS EFFECTIVE REVIEW?

Boiled down to its essentials, active effective reviewing is nothing more or less than this:

Continuous self-examination—of the essential parts of a course.

Effective review, then, consists of these two essential steps:

1. Boiling down the material of the course to its essentials, and then boiling the essentials down again and again and again, till he's mastered every word of the core meaning of that course.

2. Periodically reviewing that core material—through continuous self-examinations—till every word of its content is right at the tip of his tongue, ready to be instantly formed into an answer.

For example, mathematics is thus reduced to rules, definitions, types of problems that will be encountered in the final test, and the formulas and procedures that will solve them. Then all this essential knowledge is rehearsed, over and over again, till the correct answer to any one of the problems becomes an automatic and instant reaction.

This is the same combination of knowledge and practice

that makes a champion line backer, a top-flight golfer, or a superbly successful executive.

Once your child has reviewed his course in this way—in other words, once he has reduced it to its essentials and practiced quizzing himself on those essentials till they have become second nature—he is ready to breeze through any test that can be thrown at him on that subject.

Now, let's examine this process of review and readiness, step by step. There are three steps:

1. Weekly review.
2. Final organization of notebook.
3. Final quiz-review of the entire course.

Let's look at each one:

STEP ONE: THE WEEKLY REVIEW.

Effective review, of course, is not a once-a-semester activity. It goes on constantly, first as part of your child's day-by-day study, then to survey a larger area once every week, and then to insure understanding of the entire course at the end of the term.

We have already discussed, in Chapter 10, the first step in this continuous process. On page 103, we went over the three questions your child uses to tie in each new chapter with the one that went before. These were:

"In one sentence, what did I learn from last night's chapter?"

"How does this tie in with the chapter before?"

"What questions will I be asked on it in next week's test?"

Now, at the end of each study week, he goes one step further. Each week, he sets aside one additional half hour for review of the entire book up to that point.

During this hour, he reviews each chapter out-line in his notebook. He then ties them together—in a continuously growing over-all view of the book as a whole—with this series of questions and answers:

"How many chapters have I now read in this book?" (Using the high-school history book as our example: Three, plus an introduction.)

"What is the title of the book?" (*A History of Civilization.*)

"Does this title give the theme of the book?" (It does.) If it did not, he would then ask the question:

"What is the theme of the book?" (A history of civilization.)

"What, if any, is the title of the introduction?" ("The Uses of History.")

"What, in one sentence, is the core meaning of the introduction?" (A study of history keeps us from making the same mistakes all over again that our ancestors made.)

"What is the title of the first chapter?" ("The First Men.")

"What, in one sentence, is the core meaning of the first chapter?" (Primitive man spent almost all his time getting enough food to keep alive, until he invented agriculture.)

"What is the title of the second chapter?" ("The Near East.")

"What, in one sentence, is the core meaning of the second chapter?" (The first great civilizations in history—ruled by kings and priests and resting on slavery—were built in the Near East.)

"How does the second chapter tie in with the first?" (By showing the tremendous growth in civilization agriculture made possible, even though this civilization was enjoyed only by the few who had seized rule.)

"What is the title of the third chapter?" ("The Greeks.")

"What, in one sentence, is the core meaning of the third chapter?" (The Greeks developed the first Western civilization, inventing democracy, science, philosophy, literature, and so on.)

"How does the third chapter tie in with the second?"

(By showing the contrast between the older, king-and-priest-dominated civilizations of the Near East, and the new freedom that characterized Greek civilization.)

And so on. Chapter by chapter, every week of each course.

This never-ceasing weekly review pays off several ways. It keeps the older chapters fresh in your child's mind. It ties in each new chapter with all the material that preceded it. It gives your child an ever-growing over-all view of the course as a unified whole. It helps him get higher and higher grades in class recitations and weekly exams. It cuts down the amount of reviewing he will need to do in the last two weeks before his final exams.

And it helps him to simplify and to bring his notebook up to date, like this:

STEP TWO: THE FINAL ORGANIZATION OF HIS NOTEBOOK.

At the end of each course, when he is ready to begin his final review, your child has in his notebook:

1. A main-thought outline of every textbook chapter in the course.

2. A main-thought outline of every lecture he has been given in the course.

3. If there are any, main-thought outlines of any outside reference reading he has been assigned during the course, done in the same way as any daily reading assignment.

4. A fundamental vocabulary page for the course as a whole.

5. A list of the mistakes he has made in his daily papers during the progress of the course.

These five different parts of his notebook must now be brought together into a single final outline page for each chapter in the course.

They must be blended together—unified—with all the duplicate facts removed. They must be arranged in a single, logical order, so that every fact he has learned during the entire course *fits in perfectly,* and can be remembered—automatically—the instant he needs it.

This final blending is done in this way:

FIRST:

For each chapter, your child takes his reading notes and his lecture notes (and, if there are any, his outside reference notes) and lays them side by side.

He then takes a third sheet of paper and starts to blend them in, point by point. He starts with the chapter title, then the first main thought underneath that title, then the second, and right on down the line.

To help him with this blending task he asks himself the following questions:

"Is this fact repeated by both sources?" If so, he throws it out.

"Is this fact new?" If so, he puts it under the proper heading in his revised outline.

"Do I have to change the order of my headings because of any new facts?" Sometimes, when material from separate sources is put together, your child will find that neither one of the older outlines can contain the blended facts. In this case, he must construct a brand-new outline and order containing all the new facts in their proper relation to each other.

"Are all these facts really important—are they really main thoughts—or are some of them merely details describing other main thoughts already picked up from another source?" If so, leave them out.

These questions cause him to weigh and choose and reject. They make his mind *work.* In themselves, they are an excellent form of review. And when he is finished answering them, and shaping their answers into a final main-thought chapter outline, he will pretty well know everything there is to know about the material in that chapter.

SECOND:

Now, he goes back over his lecture notes for that chapter, and he asks himself the following questions:

"What questions will my teacher be most likely to ask about this chapter?"

"What points did she stress in her classroom lectures?"

"What information did she tell us to pay special attention to in the textbook?"

Every time he finds the answer to one of these questions in his lecture notes, he places a red check in front of that point in his revised main-thought outline. This check will serve as a signal to him when he composes his final review questions, as we will describe below.

He now throws away his reading notes, his lecture notes, and his reference notes. He has no more need for them, since they have been blended into his revised main-thought outlines.

THIRD:

Now he turns to his fundamental-vocabulary page. He removes this page from his notebook and lays it alongside his revised main-thought outlines for the course.

He goes down the vocabulary, word by word, and checks off the point in the main-thought outlines where that word is first used in the course. At that point he makes an asterisk (*) in the main-thought outline, and then writes the word and its definition at the bottom of that outline page.

He does this till he has exhausted every word in his fundamental vocabulary. He has then tied the vocabulary in with his notes, and gained a deeper understanding of both in doing it.

But he does not throw away his fundamental-vocabulary page. He continues to carry it at the back of the notebook as an instant reference if he should forget the meaning of the words as they appear in more advanced lessons.

FOURTH:

He now takes out his daily or weekly written work, and checks each one of the mistakes he has made during the entire course.

Wherever he has made a mistake, he places a red check mark against the same point in his main-thought outlines. This again reminds him to pay special attention to that point in his final review.

He now has a completely revised and ready-for-review notebook. It contains every fact he has learned from his reading, his lectures, and his reference research, all blended together into one thoroughly understood stream of thought.

In addition, he has incorporated into those outlines probable test questions, a thorough understanding of the vocabulary of the course, and review signals for every weak spot that has shown up in his work for the entire term.

He is now ready to perform one final review operation on that notebook, which will thoroughly prepare him for his final test by enabling him to anticipate 80 per cent or more of all the questions his teacher can give him, IN THE EXACT FORM THAT THAT TEACHER CAN PHRASE THEM.

STEP THREE: THE FINAL QUIZ-REVIEW OF THE ENTIRE COURSE.

Let us say that your child has begun his final revision of his notebook two weeks before the final exam. It has taken him one week to complete this revision, and thus to master the main thoughts of the entire course.

He now has one week left to prepare himself to breeze through that final exam. In the next chapter we will outline day-by-day, step-by-step procedures for that final week. Right now, however, we will see how he takes his revised notes during that final week, *and turns them into his own private test before the real test*, to make sure he knows every detail of that material.

There are two reasons, of course, why he takes this private test before the real test:

1.   Obviously, because it gives him one final chance to again review his material, to gain still deeper understanding of it, and more confidence in handling it.

2.   Because it is one thing to know the core material of a course, and quite another thing to be able quickly and accurately to answer test questions about it. To really whiz through a test, your child should be familiar with the questions he is going to be asked on that test—not only their form, but their very content. And the only way he can discover that content—outside of cheating—is to construct his own test out of the same materials his teacher will use to construct hers.

Therefore he now begins to turn his revised notes into test questions, in this way:

HOW HE MAKES UP HIS OWN TEST QUESTIONS

As we mentioned in Chapter 10, page 98, each page of your child's notes are written on one side only. He has purposely left the opposite side of those notes blank. He is now about to put that blank side to work.

Let us say that your child is going to review our sample chapter 3, *The Five Roads to Cost Reduction*. He has already revised his outline notes, to include both text and lectures ideas into one over-all outline.

He now turns that sheet of paper over and writes across the top of the blank side: *The Five Roads to Cost Reduction —Test Questions*.

He is now ready to make up his questions. In doing this, he must remember that, in his final exam, he will be given two general types of questions.

First, the *Short-Answer* questions, such as multiple-choice, true-false, fill-in, and so on.

Second, the *Essay* questions, which ask him to write a paragraph or more in answer to every question.

In order to prepare for both types of question, your child draws a horizontal line across the middle of his paper, dividing it in two.

At the top left-hand corner of the upper half, right under the over-all title, he writes: *Short-Answer Questions*:

And at the top left-hand corner of the lower half, right under his dividing line, he writes: *Essay Questions*:

He now draws a vertical line down the middle of the paper, to divide his questions from his answers. His paper now looks like this:

Five Roads to Cost Reduction — Test Questions

Short-Answer Questions	*Answers*
1.	
2.	
3.	
4.	
5.	
6.	
7.	
8.	

Essay Questions	*Answers*
1.	
2.	
3.	
4.	
5.	

He is now ready to compose his questions.

HOW HE MAKES UP HIS SHORT-ANSWER QUESTIONS

In Chapter 22, you will be shown each of the different types of short-answer questions, along with simple formulas to greatly aid your child in answering them.

Here we can touch on only a few of these types of questions, to use as examples of how your child should convert his lecture notes into a final self quiz. He proceeds in this way:

First, of course, he takes every point that his teacher has emphasized in her lectures, and converts it into a test question.

Let's say, for example, that his teacher has stressed the methods of cutting capital equipment costs in her lecture. He immediately constructs a cross-out test question on this point, and uses it as the first short-answer question on his page, like this:

Which of the following four procedures is NOT a way to cut capital equipment costs?

    a. Reducing costs of depreciation, replacement, maintenance, and interest.

    b. Holding down inventories.

    c. Operations research.

    d. Sharpening accounting procedures.

The answer, of course, is *c.* But he does not yet write in that answer. Instead, he goes on to his next question.

This next series of questions revolves around those points that he has made errors on in previous work. For each error he has made, he now composes a self-test question.

For example, let's say he had difficulty before in remembering the various ways to cut raw-material costs. He now, therefore, constructs a true-false question on just this point, in this way:

TRUE OR FALSE: Three good ways to cut raw mate-
rials costs are precise purchasing specifications, inspection
of incoming materials, and financial control of sources.

The answer, of course, is *True.* And so he goes, down
the entire list of important points, constructing a different
question for every one of the types mentioned in Chapter 22.
In this way, he becomes thoroughly familiar with each one of
these question types, *as they apply to the material he will
be tested on.*

He even uses the same procedure to make sure he knows
the exact meaning of each of the words in his fundamental
vocabulary. For example, suppose he wants to be absolutely
certain of the meaning of *Operations Research.* To test him-
self on this point, he constructs the following question:

OPERATIONS RESEARCH means most nearly: a) Cost
Accounting; b) Statistical Decision Making; c) Computer
Planning; d) Time and Motion Study.

The answer is *c.* But the construction of such a question
forces your child to think deeply about the meaning of this
new word, to compare and contrast it with the other new
terms he has learned in this course, and to dig deeper into
more and more profitable levels of understanding.

HOW HE MAKES UP HIS ESSAY QUESTIONS

The same procedure holds true on preparing his Essay
Questions. He first goes over the important points stressed
by his teacher. Then the points he has been confused on
before.

Then whatever other ideas he believes that he will be
tested on in his final exam.

For each of these he prepares an essay-type question,
such as those described in Chapter 23.

For example, on manufacturing costs, a simple essay-type question would be this:

List five ways to cut manufacturing costs.

Or, as a more complicated essay-type question:

You have just been appointed sales manager of the ABC Company. Describe five ways that you would attempt to cut their sales costs, in order, and tell why you think each of these ways would be effective.

HOW HE ANSWERS ESSAY-TYPE QUESTIONS ON HIS SELF-QUIZ PAPER

When he has written all his questions—both short-answer and essay type—down the left-hand side of his paper, your child is ready to take his own quiz and write the answers.

He does not do this the same day that he composed the questions. He waits a day, and then comes back to the quiz.

Without looking at his notes, he writes his answers. For the short-answer questions, he writes the answers completely.

For the essay-type questions, however, he does not write a complete answer. Instead, he *outlines* each of the answers as briefly as possible, and does not take the time to actually write in the outline as he would do in an actual test.

He is only trying to develop the main ideas for his answer, and the order in which he would arrange them. Once he has this, he can be satisfied, and go on to the next question.

For example, in the essay question two, about the sales manager position described on the last page, your child would outline his answer in this way:

WAY TO CUT COST:	REASON WHY:
1. *Advertising.*	1. *Biggest cost today.*
2. *Warehousing.*	2. *Greatest per-cent improvement.*
3. *Transportation.*	3. *Big waste in most co's.*
4. *Direct Sales.*	4. *Fat usually creeps in.*
5. *New Specialists.*	5. *May be cut entirely.*

HOW HE REVIEWS HIS SELF-QUIZZES

Once he has taken the test, your child grades himself right or wrong, just as his teacher would. Those answers that he has right he forgets until the last day before the test.

Those answers that he has wrong he reviews again the next day, in this way:

He places a red check mark in front of the question he has missed. The next day, he takes out the self-quiz again, covers the answer side with a sheet of fresh paper, and tries to answer the question again.

If he gets it correctly this second time, he forgets it till the last day before the test.

If he misses it again, he rereads his notes, and then turns back to the original textbook material and rereads it again. If he still does not understand it after this rereading, he immediately speaks to his teacher about it, going over it with her until he is absolutely sure of it.

Remember, his goal—and your goal—is to make certain that he understands every important idea in the course well enough to allow him to answer any question on it that can be thrown at him. You can accept nothing less.

WHAT THESE SELF-QUIZZES WILL DO FOR YOUR CHILD

If he has done them correctly, when your child is through with these self-quizzes, he has accomplished the dream of every student who has ever walked down a classroom aisle to take a final exam:

He will actually know the examination questions in advance!

You see, his teacher, in preparing her final tests, has no more material to choose from than your child. Both your child and his teacher will have to concentrate on the same broad ideas and important details as the sources for their test material.

Therefore, to a surprisingly large extent, they must come up with exactly the same questions.

Think of the thrill your child will get when he marches into his final exam room and finds dozens of the same exact test questions waiting there for him—*with the correct answers perfectly stored away in his head, ready to spring onto the paper.*

Think of the headstart this will give him over his more poorly prepared classmates. Think of the tremendous burst of confidence this will raise in him—to completely erase any nervousness he might have brought into the room with him, to carry him right through every question on the test, with his mind already revved up to full working power, pulling out correct answers as fast as he can write them down on the page.

Isn't this a wonderful gift to give your child, for only a few disciplined minutes each day, the final week before he takes that test?

In summary:

A truly effective review is continuous self-examination of the essential parts of a course.

This continuous self-examination goes on every week of the course, right up until the final examination. It takes place in three stages:

1. *The weekly review.* Where the child ties in every new chapter he has learned during the week with all the material that has gone before it. In this way he gains a constantly growing over-all view of the course, with all its important parts fresh in his mind.

2. *The final organization of his notebook.* Where he organizes and blends in all the information he has received during the course—from his textbook, his lectures, his outside reference work, his vocabulary building, and his error feedback. From this blending, he gains a final unified outline of the backbone ideas of the course, all at his fingertips for instant reference.

3. *The final quiz-review of the entire course.* Where he writes his own final exam on the important ideas he has learned in the entire term, becoming familiar and at ease with both the content and form of such an exam. From this final self-quiz, he gains dozens of the actual questions that will be asked of him in his final exam, plus the confidence that he can answer any other question that can be asked of him.

With this solid bedrock foundation of review to back him, we now turn to the final examinations themselves, and see dozens of simple ways to improve his performance in them.

PART SIX

HOW TO BREEZE THROUGH TESTS

CHAPTER 22

THE WEEK BEFORE THE TEST—
WHAT TO DO AND WHAT NOT TO DO

The final goal of all your child's planning—all his work, all his learning and relearning and review—is one or two or three hours in a closed room, proving his year's accomplishment, in the educational ritual called the *test*, which separates the winners from the losers.

Some parents object to tests as unfair, anxiety causing, and not really proving anything. This is untrue. Life is a series of tests. Some are written, some are verbal, some are economic or social or moral.

In any case, your child had better get used to passing all of them now. The winner's circle is an entirely different world from the habitat of the also-ran.

THE FIRST GREAT STEP IN IM-
PROVING ANY CHILD'S TEST GRADES

Test performance can be improved, just as performance in any competitive activity can be improved. And as in developing any other skill, the two magic ingredients are:
1. Knowledge, and
2. Practice.

And as in any other form of pay-off competition, there is always one great enemy to face and overcome: fear.

Fear destroys students in tests, just as fear can destroy their parents in later life. The student who tenses up, panics, loses all his carefully stored information the moment he faces the test paper, is beaten before he even tries.

Therefore the first step in preparing your child to master any kind of examination is to always ask this question:

What causes fear in a test situation?

The answer is twofold:

1. Not knowing the material upon which he is going to be tested.

2. Not knowing the forms and procedures by which he will be tested.

Either one of these two test fears can knock your child right out of a top grade. They can cause a performance 30 per cent to 50 per cent *less* than your child is really capable of giving.

You must prevent this loss. But how?

Quite simply, really, in these three tested and proved ways:

1. Preparation.
2. Familiarity.
3. Practice.

Let's discuss each of them in turn:

FIRST, of course, preparation. Knowing the material of his course. Knowing it backward and forward. Boiling it down into its main ideas; arranging those main ideas in the right logical order so that one automatically suggests another; and filing those ideas away in his mind so permanently that they spring to his tongue or his hand the very instant he needs them.

This preparation for the final exam begins the very first day he enters class. This book has been a step-by-step blueprint on how to conduct that preparation, how to make it as thorough as possible, and how to make it instantly available again, at the moment of pay-off.

FAMILIARITY BREEDS CONTEMPT— WITH TESTS AS WELL AS PEOPLE

SECOND, after your child has mastered the content of his course, he must then equally master the forms by which he will be questioned about it.

Tests frighten children by their very appearance. The sight of a strange new way to ask a question can cause a child to miss an answer that he knows perfectly well. Questions, as every student knows, can be tricky. *Your job is to take the trickery out of them before he encounters them in the test room.*

This demands that you sit down with your child and show him, one by one, the types of questions he will be asked in his exams. You show him how these questions are built, how to read them, what he must do to solve them, and how they themselves can help him solve them.

Then you go over the same type of question two, three, four or more times, until he is as familiar with the way to work out the answer to that question, as he is with the way to write his own name.

Your goal is simple. You must make absolutely certain that your child is never, in his entire school career, confronted with a type or form of question that he has never seen before.

The moment he glances at that question, its form must be so familiar to him that he knows automatically, without a second thought, the procedure by which he will answer it. He must be able to concentrate instantly on the content of that question, to devote his full energies to retrieving the material that will answer it, without giving the form of the question a second thought.

This is what the next two chapters will do for your child. First, every type of short-answer question now in popular use. Then every type of essay question.

To build into his test-taking personality familiarity—his second great weapon against fear.

PRACTICE MAKES PERFECT—PERFECT KNOWLEDGE, PERFECT CONFIDENCE

THIRD, and finally, once he knows his course material, and once he knows the form or type of questions he's going to be asked about it, then he puts the two together in constant, continuous *practice*.

Your child takes tests from the very first day he opens a book. *You* test him every single night in your Parent Achievement Check. *He* tests himself, with every main-thought outline he writes each night, every tie-in talk he has each morning, every weekly review he finishes each Friday.

Every time he does a problem in mathematics, he tests himself. Every time he corrects an error in his homework, he retests himself.

Every day, he subjects himself to a barrage of questions. Till questions become second nature to him. Till he can smell a possible test question on a printed page a mile away. *Till his mind becomes one great razor-sharp instrument for asking and answering questions. And, at that moment, you can take credit not only for top grades, but for having developed a truly educated child.*

Education is, in the last analysis, the ability to ask and answer questions. It is active knowledge seeking out new knowledge to deepen its understanding. It is thought in action, able to learn, to solve, to build. It is probably the most precious gift, after love, that you will ever hand on to your child.

HIS STUDY SCHEDULE FOR THE FINAL TWO WEEKS BEFORE THE TEST

Fortunately, this continuous question-and-answer approach to education keeps your child constantly reviewing, constantly prepared for whatever tests he may encounter. Therefore, as we have seen in the previous chapter, his formal preparation for his final test requires much less time than that needed by his less-organized classmates.

Once again, however, for these final two weeks, he draws up a definite plan of attack. To get the greatest benefit out of every study hour, for every course, he does this:

1. He divides the last two weeks before the final test up into *six* working days. He then decides how many hours he will have in each working day to devote to study—let us say three hours a day. This gives him eighteen working hours per week for the last two weeks.

2. He then takes the number of courses he will have to study for. Let us say there are four. Thus four courses into eighteen hours each week gives him four hours plus during the week to devote to each course.

If one course is slightly harder than the others, he devotes an extra hour or two to it. But in any case he sets up a definite allotment of study hours for each of his courses before he begins his final review for them.

3. During the first week, his review will consist of rewriting and blending his notes, as detailed in Chapter 20. Let us assume that he spends all his allotted four hours per course in that first week, on this active rewriting of his notes.

4. During his final week, he devotes his first two hours to taking those notes and writing his own final exam about them.

He then devotes the third hour—a day later—to taking this self-exam, checking his weak points, reviewing the material that will deepen his understanding of them, and marking each still-troublesome idea for one last review the next day.

THE FINAL HOUR OF PREPARATION—
PREFERABLY WITH A FRIEND

He is now ready for his last self-exam. He will take it on this basis:

What your child has done up to this point has been a process of condensation, of boiling down the material of each course in two ways:

First, to its main thoughts, its backbone meaning, its important ideas that he must be tested upon.

Second, to each one of those main ideas that is particularly hard for him. That he does not quite understand. That he cannot answer as quickly and accurately as he can all the others.

Throughout his hours and hours of self-examination, he has gradually mastered and put aside those important ideas that he thoroughly understands. In his two weeks of final review, he first refreshed his memory on these well-known facts, and then tested his ability to recall them easily and completely.

Now he has put them aside. He *knows* that he can answer any test question about them.

This leaves him, in this last hour of review, face to face with his own particular trouble-makers.

These are the facts upon which he is vague. The problems he cannot solve automatically. The questions that might trip him up without this one final hour of mastery.

Now he attacks them directly, in every form, shape, and way that both he and you can think of.

If possible, *you* should be with him in this final hour of mastery. Your job here is that of question asker. You should take every one of those trouble-makers in turn, and invent five, six, seven different approaches, different questions to sharpen his mind about them.

For example, take the first of them, and first ask a true-false question about it. Then switch to a multiple-answer question. Then to cross-out question. Then to a comparison-contrast question.

Ask as many questions as you can think up about that one trouble-maker. Keep asking till the right answer becomes automatic on your child's lips. Then go on to the next trouble-maker and do the same.

Of course, familiarity with the subject matter will greatly aid this final, intensive quiz. Therefore, for at least this last hour, it is advisable that your child review this material with another serious friend.

Let us assume that both children have prepared for their final exams in approximately the same way described above. In this case, each child has prepared his own self-quiz on the same material.

But no two minds think alike, and one may have picked some vital point that the other has neglected. Therefore, for the first half hour of this last review hour, have them give each other their own quizzes.

This should be done orally. Fast. With the answers springing from their lips almost the instant the questions are finished.

Many of the questions your child will have already anticipated, almost phrased exactly the same. Realizing this will give his confidence a huge boost.

Other questions will be slight rephrases, or on different points than he might have stressed. This will give him a chance to pull the material out of his mind, to become accustomed to turning questions into answers automatically.

When the quizzes are over, each child then turns to his trouble-makers. They intensively quiz each other on just these points. They discuss their answers. The two points of view merge. New insights are gained by each. This may be the final push that leads your child to absolute understanding of a point that has been bothering him since the beginning of the school year, so he can now file it away and forget it.

HOW TO MAKE SURE HE REMEMBERS HIS MEMORY WORK WHEN HE GOES INTO THE EXAMINATION ROOM

In addition to this backbone meaning of his course, your child will be confronted from time to time with other facts, equally important, which he must memorize exactly, detail for detail. These may be mathematical formulas, history dates, equations in chemistry or physics, and so on.

With such facts, his problem is one of sheer memorization. He must have them engraved on his memory by the time he walks into the exam room. He can do this most easily by following the following procedure:

1. He buys a packet of 5½ by 8 inch library cards that fit into his pocket. Each formula he wants to memorize he writes down exactly on one of these cards. He uses a separate card for each formula he wishes to retain.

2. On the front of each card he writes down the name of the formula. For example, he might write on the front of one card:

To find the area of a circle.

3. On the back of the card, he writes the formula itself. For example: $A = \pi R^2$

4. He carries these cards with him to every class. Whenever he has a spare moment, he pulls them out, looks at the identifying name on the front, and tries to recite the exact formula from memory. He then turns the card over to see if he is correct.

5. When he has repeated the correct formula three times from memory, he takes the card and files it away till the week before the final test. If he cannot repeat it three times from memory, he continues in this way:

6. The final week before the test, each night he takes each of the difficult formulas and lays them in a pile face up on his study table. He reads their names one by one, and then writes down their formulas on a piece of paper. Then he checks his answers against the backs of his cards.

7. Right or wrong, he continues this writing and checking procedure for five nights before the final test.

8. On the day of the test, in the morning before he leaves for school, he runs through the hardest of the cards again—writing and then checking and, if necessary, correcting.

9. He then takes these hard-formula cards with him to school. When he reaches the test room, one minute before the test begins, he takes out the cards again. He takes them

one by one, and this time he writes the formula down on the face of the card, underneath the name.

10.   He then checks the back of the card to see if he is right. If he is right, he underlines the correct formula on the front of the card. If he is wrong, he writes down the correct formula on the front of the card once more.

11.   Then he tears up the cards and throws them away. He walks directly to his desk, takes the exam paper as soon as it is given to him, and writes the correct formulas in its margin.

He now has the correct formulas at his fingertips, ready to go to work for him in the examination.

THE NIGHT BEFORE THE TEST

One last note on this final week before the test. We have tried to prepare your child as perfectly as humanly possible for this examination. We therefore assume that he is ready to take this final exam—as only one of a series of examinations that he has been taking all year long—the day before the test.

Therefore any final study the night before the test would only be wasted effort. Let him relax that night. A good dinner, perhaps an early movie or soda with the family, then a sound night's sleep.

He will forget nothing in that final night's relaxation. He is prepared. He can take the test the next morning with absolute self-confidence.

In summary:

There are three simple secrets to achieving the absolute top grades in any test your child will ever take during his entire life:

1. Preparation—to master the content of the course.
2. Familiarity—with the types of questions that he will be asked.
3. Practice—to combine this content and form into a flawless routine of instant-precision answers.

After a final week of such practice, your child should be able to walk into his examination room with complete self-assurance.

To help him do this, we now examine the type of questions he will be asked, and how he can avoid any pitfalls they may present for him.

CHAPTER 23

TYPES OF SHORT-ANSWER TESTS AND
HOW TO MASTER THEM

The most frequent type of test your child will encounter is the objective or short-answer or write-in test.

Such tests—and there are at least ten different forms of them—present a series of short questions to your child, and then ask him to give a short answer to each. Often this answer is no more than a single word, a yes or a no, or a check mark in the proper space.

Thus these short-answer tests require no writing skill on the part of your child. During an entire test, he may not write a single sentence.

Because of this, many parents falsely believe that these write-in tests are nothing but measurements of memory, that they do not require their children to think, and that the child with the strongest memory is the child who will score highest on such tests.

Nothing could be further from the truth. A working knowledge of the facts—memorization—is only the first step required to score top marks on such short-answer tests. Assuming that your child is thoroughly prepared in the content of his course—as we have tried to achieve in this book—he must also bring to the test at least three other vital skills.

IF HE WANTS TOP GRADES ON THESE OBJEC-TIVE TESTS, YOUR CHILD MUST BE ABLE TO:

1. *Read with Precision.* Short-answer tests are tricky tests. They are designed to expose the sloppy thinker and the

221

careless reader. Time after time, their most heavily graded questions will turn on a single key word.

For example, take this true-false question in American history:

True or false: Many pioneers died in Death Valley where the climate is hot and humid.

This statement is perfectly true right up until the last word, which is false, and which therefore turns the entire statement false.

Therefore your child must be able to pick out those key words at a glance, understand whether they ask a straight or twisted question, and thus avoid the traps that destroy his unwary classmates.

2. *Make Judgments Between Right and Wrong Choices.* Most short-answer tests do not merely ask for the right answer to a question; instead they furnish your child with a series of possible answers—both right and wrong—to that question.

For example, take this typical question from an English vocabulary test:

Choose the answer which is most nearly OPPOSITE in meaning to the word in capital letters.

1. UNFIT: (A) tight (B) qualified (C) chosen (D) serene (E) necessary.

With such a question, it is equally as important to be able to eliminate the wrong answers (*tight, chosen, serene, necessary*) as it is to be able to select *qualified* as the right answer.

This calls for *test judgment.* In a moment, we'll show you how your child can develop it.

3. *Reason a Problem, Step by Step, to Its Conclusion.* And always, of course, in *every* test, on *every* question, your child must be able to think. To work from the facts that are given to the facts that are asked for.

For example, take this problem from a College Entrance Exam:

Fill in the next two numbers in the following progression: 5 9 13 17 21 25 29 — —

Here your child must be able to find a pattern (that each number is 4 higher than the number before it), and project that pattern to come up with the correct answers, 33 and 37.

And he must be able to set up these reasoning patterns, and put them to use, almost as fast as he can run his eyes over the question. We'll show you how in a moment.

So there you have them. The three *test abilities* your child must bring to every examination:

1. The ability to read with precision.

2. The ability to make judgments between right and wrong choices.

3. The ability to reason through a problem.

Now, let's see how we can sharpen each one of those abilities in your child.

Let's turn to the *ten* most common types of short-answer questions and examine them one by one.

Let's see how some of these questions demand emphasis on one ability, and other questions require another.

And let's learn the simple techniques that *double* the power of your child's abilities on each one of these questions, whenever he encounters them on a test.

TYPE OF SHORT-ANSWER QUESTION 1: TRUE-FALSE

DEFINITION: The true-false question is the simplest form of short-answer question. It presents a statement to your child, and asks him to tell whether he considers that statement true or false.

WHAT IT LOOKS LIKE: There are several forms of the true-false question. They look like this:

A. Straight form:

George Washington was the first president of the United States. _____.

Here the words *true* or *false* are to be written in after the statement.

B.   Circle form:

T   F   George Washington was the first president of the United States.

Here your child circles the T or F, or underlines them, or checks them, or in some other positive way marks his choice.

C.   Cross-out form:

Here the question looks the same as the circle form shown above:

T   F   George Washington was the first . president of the United States.

However, in this test, the *instructions* for the test indicate that your child should *cross out* the *wrong* choice, rather than mark the right choice. Here, for example, he would *cross out* the F, rather than underline the T.

It is essential that your child read the instructions thoroughly at the beginning of *every* test, to avoid any confusion between these two types of true-false choices. A single overlooked word here can ruin an entire year of study.

D.   Separate-answer-sheet form:

Here the question is written on one paper, and space for the answer is given on a separate answer sheet, which is usually graded by a machine.

Each question and answer are, of course, numbered, and look like this:

On the question sheet:

17.   *George Washington was the first president of the United States.*

On the answer sheet:

            T   F

17. || ||

With such a test, neatness and precision again become

crucial. It is incredible how many students lose grades on such tests, simply because they place the right answer in the wrong space. It is your job to make sure that such waste can never happen with your child.

HOW TO MASTER IT

A true-false question is either completely right or it's wrong. In other words, every single word in the question must be utterly true, or the entire question is false. If there is one exception to the statement, it's false.

Therefore every word counts. One tiny word, anywhere in the statement, can turn it from true to false. Here, precision reading pays off. Your child should underline the key words of each statement in this way:

Harry S. Truman, born in *Independence*, Missouri, was 33rd president of the United States.

Here are two key facts that must be true to make the statement true. Truman must have been the 33rd president of the United States, not the 32nd or 34th. And he must have been born in *Independence*, not in Saint Louis or Kansas City.

Since the second statement is false—since President Truman was not born in Independence—the question is answered false.

The procedure for answering a true-false question, therefore, is this:

1. Read the statement carefully.
2. Read it again, underlining the key words.
3. Determine whether each key word, each key fact, is true or false.
4. If any key fact is wrong, the statement is wrong. Only if all the key facts are correct can the statement be true.

WHAT TO WATCH OUT FOR

In a true-false test your child should always be suspicious of flat statements that allow no exceptions. They are probably false. Tip-offs include such words as:

All	Never
Always	Invariably
No	Any
None	Absolutely
Every	

When your child sees such a word in a true-false question, he should automatically mark it false unless he is absolutely sure that there is no exception to its rule.

On the other hand, the following moderate words in a true-false question are usually tip-offs that the question is true:

Usually
On the average
Some
Many
Often

When he encounters such words, your child should mark the question true, unless he finds a key fact later in the statement that twists it false.

TYPE OF SHORT-ANSWER QUESTION 2: MULTIPLE CHOICE

DEFINITION: The multiple-choice test lists a number of possible answers after each of its questions. One of these answers is right; the rest are wrong. It is your child's task to choose the correct one.

WHAT IT LOOKS LIKE: The multiple-choice question may list its answers on the same line as the question itself, like this:

1. *American fighter planes are usually armed with machine guns of* 22   30   32   45   50   57 *caliber.*

Or it may list the answers on separate lines, like this:

2. *An efficient student—*

    a.   Studies with the radio volume lowered.

   b. Studies at least two hours for every hour spent in class each week.

   c. Does most of his reviewing just prior to an examination.

   d. Does not make notations in his textbook.

It may list the answers as part of an incomplete statement, as in the examples above. Or it may ask a complete question, with separate answers listed below it, like this:

   3. *Which of the following is not an effective study habit?*

    a. Studying in the same place each day.

    b. Revising notes immediately after lectures.

    c. Having a separate notebook for each class.

HOW TO MASTER IT

 Whatever its form, the multiple-choice question forces your child to choose and reject. And it does not make this choice easy. In fact, it often deliberately confuses, by furnishing answers that are designed *to look near-correct,* and thus throw your child off the track.

 For example, take this question from a vocabulary test. It asks your child to choose the definition that is nearest in meaning to the first capitalized word.

   4. *IMPOSTURE — A: excessive burden. B: stooping position. C: fraud. D: handicap.*

 In this case, the correct answer is *C: fraud.* But there are two deliberately misleading clues in the question designed to draw your child away from that correct answer, if he does not know it thoroughly.

 The first is *A: excessive burden,* which is a definition of IMPOSITION, a word similar to imposture.

 The second is *B: stooping position,* which plays on a possible misreading by your child of the -POSTURE part of the question word.

 Because of these built-in traps, a definite step-by-step

technique is essential in answering multiple-choice questions. Let's examine that technique, right now:

STEP ONE: ANTICIPATE THE ANSWER.

In multiple-choice questions like examples 1 and 4 above, where the question or incomplete-statement part makes sense by itself alone, without your child reading on to the list of possible answers, train him to do this:

FIRST: Read the first part of the question (for example, in 4, he reads just the word *IMPOSTURE*) and then stop.

SECOND: *Before* he goes on to the list of possible answers, have him lightly jot down on the side of the paper what he believes is the correct answer.

(For example, he may immediately realize that IMPOSTURE means fakery or fraud. Or he may associate it with IMPOSTOR, a man who is a fraud. Let him lightly sketch the idea of fraud next to the answer, and then go on with the next step.)

THIRD: Then he looks for what he believes is the correct answer among the list of possible answers printed on the test.

(For example, when he sees *C: fraud* in the list of answers, he can be almost certain that he has it right.)

So his procedure in Step One—anticipating the answer—is first to read the question part of the statement, then jot down what he thinks is the correct answer, then look for that correct answer in the list of possible answers that completes the question.

Now, in examples 2 and 3 above, this technique must be altered slightly. Here the question part does not make sense by itself (for example, in 2, it says only: *"An efficient student—"*)

Therefore he must read on, over each of the possible answers, *making a light pencil check mark on the answer he believes is correct as soon as he reads it.*

(For example, he reads on to

1.   *Studies with the radio volume lowered.*

Which he does not believe is correct. So he goes on to:

   2.   *Studies at least two hours for every hour spent in class.*)

This he believes is the correct answer. So he checks it lightly as his first choice, and goes on to the second step, which is:

STEP TWO: READ EVERY POSSIBLE ANSWER.

Now, once your child has anticipated what he believes is the correct answer, he must make absolutely sure that he is right. He does this by a process of checking and elimination.

To begin this check, he now reads every possible answer on the list.

(For example, in example 2 above, he goes on to read:

   3.   *Does most of his reviewing just prior to an examination.*

And he also reads:

   4.   *Does not make notations in his textbook.*)

STEP THREE: ELIMINATE THE WRONG ANSWERS.

Now, as he reads each of these other possible answers, he eliminates them one by one as being incorrect. Only when he has rejected all other answers except the correct one—only when he has proved to himself that they are wrong—can he be certain that his choice is absolutely right.

To do this, he must give himself a reason why each rejected answer is wrong. Let's see how he does this in example 2 above:

(He reads:

   1.   *Studies with the radio volume lowered.*

He immediately rejects this answer as wrong, because the good student does not have the radio on when he studies at all. He then reads:

   3.   *Does most of his reviewing just prior to an examination.*

Which is wrong because review is a continuous process,

starting the first day of study. And then he finishes the list by reading:

4. *Does not make notations in his textbook.*

Which is again wrong because the good student will underline in his textbook the essence of each chapter before he transfers that essence to his notebook.)

He has now cross-checked his answer. He has anticipated the one correct answer; he has read all the others; and he has rejected them as wrong. He is now sure he is right.

STEP FOUR: MARK DOWN THE CORRECT ANSWER.

He then marks down this correct answer, and goes on to the next question.

HOW HE CAN MAKE A MULTIPLE-CHOICE QUESTION HELP HIM FIND THE CORRECT ANSWER, IF HE'S NOT SURE OF IT HIMSELF

If your child is well prepared, the technique outlined above will make him absolutely certain that he has the correct answer to over 90 per cent of all multiple-choice questions.

However, there will always be a question or two in every test where your child is not sure of the correct answer. He may be confused; he may have temporarily forgotten it; he may need just a slight nudge to regain it again.

In this case, the question itself may help him clear up this confusion and point the way to the correct answer. Let's examine some of the techniques by which he can use the structure or make-up of that question to help him find the correct answer.

ELIMINATE THE WRONG ANSWERS FIRST.

In most multiple-choice questions, your child may not be sure which of the possible answers is correct, but he probably can tell that some of them are definitely wrong. In this case, since it is easier to choose among two answers than five, he should immediately cross out the answers that he knows are wrong.

(For example, in 4 above, he may be confused between whether *IMPOSTURE* is *A: an excessive burden* or *C: a fraud.* But he is sure that it is not *B: a stooping position* or *D: a handicap.* So he eliminates these two possibilities, and thus focuses his attention on the two remaining possibilities, to which he now applies the following techniques.)

REPHRASE THE QUESTION.

Often the memory-prod your child needs to come up with the right answer can be furnished by rephrasing the question. By turning a positive question into a negative one, by turning a noun asked for into a verb, or any other way of gaining a new slant on the question.

For example, in 4 above, instead of wrestling with IM-POSTURE, the act of defrauding, your child may try changing the word into IMPOSTOR, a person who defrauds. Here he has a word that is far more familiar to him, and that immediately clears up any question he might have had about whether the word could mean *an excessive burden.*

In the same way, in example 3 above, if he was torn between answers 2 and 3, your child would rephrase the question in this way:

Which of the following IS an effective study habit?

2. *Revising notes immediately after class?* YES.

3. *Having a separate notebook for each class?* NO.

The answer becomes obvious immediately. By simply stating the OPPOSITE to the original question asked, the correct answer is thrown into clear focus.

TRY TO ELIMINATE EXTREMES.

Some multiple-choice questions, such as example 1 above, will have a scale of answers. This question asks your child to complete the statement:

American fighter planes are usually armed with machine guns of 22 30 32 45 50 54 *caliber.*

On scale question like this one, if he is not certain of

the correct answer at once, your child should start to work on the question by trying to eliminate the 22 and 54 caliber extremes. In most cases, these will be incorrect, and will leave him only four possible answers to choose from, rather than six.

LOOK FOR INTERNAL CLUES.

Many multiple-choice questions help your child answer them, simply because of their own construction. In some cases this construction eliminates certain possible answers; in others it points almost directly to the correct answer. Let us look at an example of each.

Which of the following were in part results of the immigration policy of the United States during the latter half of the nineteenth century?

1 — *supply of cheap labor.*
2 — *growth of urban populations.*
3 — *opposition of organized labor to immigration policy.*
4 — *decline in birth rate.*
(A)   *1 and 2 only.*
(B)   *1 and 3 only.*
(C)   *1, 2 and 3 only.*
(D)   *1, 2 and 4 only.*
(E)   *1, 2, 3 and 4.*

Notice that all five possible answers include result 1— *supply of cheap labor.* Therefore, instantly, your child can assume that this answer is correct, and use it as a test-furnished clue to help him choose the correct answer from the other choices.

In this case, of course, the fact that the immigration policy increased the supply of labor also meant that it increased the growth of urban populations, and that it naturally produced an opposition of organized labor to this incoming cheap-labor supply. It did not, however, decrease in any way the birth rate, but probably raised it.

Therefore, by using the first possible correct answer as

a clue, and logically applying its information to the remaining answers, your child pulled out the final answer, even though he did not know that answer when he first read the question.

The same technique of making the question furnish its own answer applies in the following example:

The action of "A Tale of Two Cities" takes place in:

1 — *Glasgow and London*
2 — *New York and Paris*
3 — *Vienna and Rome*
4 — *Paris and London*
5 — *Dublin and Edinburgh*

Here your child simply notices that only two cities are mentioned *twice* in the list of possible answers—*Paris* and *London*. Since these cities are mentioned twice—once together and once each with a third city to catch the unwary or careless student—it's highly probable that they are the correct answers. Which they are.

LOOK FOR SIGNS OF EXTRA CARE.

Finally, if he is stumped on a multiple-choice question, your child should always check to see if one of the possible answers is longer, or in a different vocabulary, or in any other way has had extra care spent on it, than the other answers in the list. If it has, this is a definite clue that it might be the correct answer.

For example, take this question from a College Board test on chemistry:

The burning of gasoline in an automobile involves all of the following EXCEPT

(A) *reduction*
(B) *decomposition*
(C) *an exothermic reaction*
(D) *oxidation*
(E) *conversion of matter to energy*

Here two separate signs of extra care coincide to point out answer (E) as the correct one. First, it is much longer than the other answers. Second, it uses a different vocabulary —talking in plain English rather than technical terms.

These two clues should lead your child to strongly suspect that answer (E) is the one he is looking for. Which it is.

Of course, all these techniques of making the question help your child answer it are merely supplements to his own preparation and knowledge. Ideally, they should be used merely to help him check the fact that he knows the right answer, or as memory prods to help him over a temporary block in retrieving that answer from his storehouse of knowledge. They are never substitutes for study or ability.

A NOTE ON THE MASTERY OF MULTIPLE-CHOICE QUESTIONS IN VOCABULARY TESTS

Most vocabulary tests—and they are extremely important to your child's progress in both his schoolwork and on intelligence tests—are phrased in the form of multiple-choice questions.

These questions will either ask for synonyms (words that mean the same as the given word) or antonyms (words that mean the opposite of the given word). The synonym question is given in example 4 above. An antonym question is given in the example below:

Choose the lettered word which is most nearly OPPO-SITE in meaning to the word in capital letters.

UNFIT: (A) tight (B) qualified (C) chosen (D) serene (E) necessary.

Such an antonym question is really two questions in one, and deserves a special technique of its own to solve it. Here it is:

STEP ONE: THINK OF A SYNONYM FOR THE WORD.

The moment your child reads the capitalized word, he should stop without reading on. *Before* he looks at the list of possible answers, he should jot down his synonym. For example, in this case, he might think of *not fit, incapable, unqualified*.

STEP TWO: THINK OF THE OPPOSITE OF THAT SYNONYM.

Now—again *before* he reads the list of possible answers —your child jots down the *opposite* of his synonym on his paper. He writes *fit, capable, qualified*.

STEP THREE: READ THE ANSWER LIST, AND ELIMINATE AND CHOOSE.

He now reads each possible answer in turn, comparing it with his own idea. He rejects *tight*; is delighted to find the exact word he had anticipated, *qualified*, as the second possible answer; then goes on to eliminate *chosen, serene*, and *necessary* as a final check.

In this step-by-step way, such problems become simple, and confusion and trickery are both side-stepped.

One more clue to help your child solve these vocabulary tests. The word he is looking for in the answer list should be the same grammatical term as the given, capitalized word.

If the given word is a noun, the correct answer should be a noun. If the given word is a verb, the correct answer should be a verb. And so on.

If, on the other hand, one of the possible answers is a different grammatical term (for instance, a verb when the given word is a noun), then it should be automatically eliminated as incorrect.

TYPE OF SHORT-ANSWER QUESTION 3: COMPLETION

DEFINITION: A completion question is similar to a multiple-choice question. But instead of choosing the correct answer from a list of perhaps five possibilities, your child must provide the answer himself, writing it in the blank space provided on the test form.

WHAT IT LOOKS LIKE: A completion question that asked

for the same information as example 1 of the multiple-choice questions given above would look like this:

American fighter planes are usually armed with machine guns of —— caliber.

HOW TO MASTER IT

A completion question demands knowledge and preparation. Your child must know the answer when he walks into the test room. The only clues that will be given to him—and these are very slight—are the following:

TIPS ON ANSWERING THEM

1. The number of blanks that are furnished. For example, in this question:

In the lungs the blood exchanges —— —— for oxygen.

The two blank spaces indicate that two words will make up the correct answer. This may give your child the hint he needs to retrieve *carbon dioxide* from his memory storehouse.

2. *A* or *an* in front of the blank spaces. For example, in this question:

A flying machine without wings is called an ——.

The *an* clue may lead your child to rule out *helicopter* and come up with *autogiro* as the correct answer.

3. A verb clue as to single or plural answers.

None of these clues, however, is, as with any other type of question, a substitute for sheer hard preparation.

TYPE OF SHORT-ANSWER QUESTION 4: ENUMERATION

DEFINITION: An enumeration question asks your child to *list* a number of series of facts. It does not require the list to be given in any set order. It usually begins with the words *list* or *name*.

WHAT IT LOOKS LIKE: For example:

List the members of the President's cabinet.

HOW TO MASTER IT

Here again, preparation is critical. If you know that your child will be given enumeration questions on his tests, help prepare him for them by:

1. Giving such questions on his review self-examinations. And make sure that he gets *all* the items in the series down on the paper.

2. In a series enumeration question, have him *number* the items in the series. Thus, if he knows that there are *ten* members of the President's cabinet, he will not list only nine on his exam paper by mistake, and forget to put in the tenth.

TYPE OF SHORT-ANSWER QUESTION 5: SEQUENCE

DEFINITION: A sequence question asks your child to list a series of facts in their proper order. Usually this will be the order in which historical events happened.

Or, as a combination of the sequence and multiple-choice type of questions, your child may be supplied with a list of events and asked to number them according to time.

WHAT IT LOOKS LIKE: The first form would be as simple as this:

List the first five Presidents of the United States in the order that they held office.

The second form would look like this:

Number the following events in order of sequence.

—*Congress of Berlin.*

—*Monroe Doctrine.*

—*Boxer Rebellion.*

—*Mexican War.*

HOW TO MASTER THEM.

In dealing with the second form, there are two tactics to follow:

1. Look for the first and last items of the series and

number them first. Then look for the second and next-to-last items. And so on. In this way, your child is again getting rid of the *extremes* first. And in this way narrowing down his area of choice and possibilities of making a mistake.

2. Number those items of which you are sure first. With a long list, he should take a piece of scratch paper, and recreate the list on it, putting down the items of which he is sure in their proper positions, and then simply using the other items to fill in the gaps.

TYPE OF SHORT-ANSWER QUESTION 6: MATCHING

DEFINITION: A matching question usually consists of two lists of items placed side by side. Your child is required to match the items on one list with the items on the other by marking the numbers from the first list in the spaces provided in front of the second.

WHAT IT LOOKS LIKE: *Write the letter of each of the cities in front of the state of which it is the capital.*

—South Dakota	A.	Frankfort
—Kentucky	B.	Pierre
—California	C.	Omaha
—Nevada	D.	Sacramento
—Nebraska	E.	Carson City

HOW TO MASTER IT

Again, elimination of known answers is the key. There are two quick methods of doing this:

1. Your child should run light pencil lines between those items on the first and second lists that he is absolutely sure of.

2. Have him cross off an item in the second list as soon as he marks its letter on the first list.

In this way he eliminates the sure answers first and is able to concentrate his attention on the one or two remaining items that need more prodding without being confused.

Here again, he must remember that *tests also teach*. They give information as well as demand it. Many clues are contained in a matching question that will help him pull out the correct answer.

For example, in the question above, he may not know that Carson City is the capital of Nevada, but he may know that it is a city in that state. The mere fact that it is mentioned in a list of state capitals then tells him all he needs to know to answer the question correctly.

TYPE OF SHORT-ANSWER QUESTION 7: CROSS OUT

DEFINITION: A cross-out question is one that asks your child to eliminate the *wrong* item in a series. For example:

WHAT IT LOOKS LIKE: *Cross out the numbers that do not belong in the following series*:

5   10   20   40   50   60   80   160   320

HOW TO MASTER IT

Cross-out questions are difficult for most students because they are really two-part questions and must be done one part at a time. If your child tries to do both parts at the same time, or just plunges hopelessly into the question without an organized technique, he will become immediately lost.

With technique, however, the cross-out question is really quite simple. Here is the proper procedure:

STEP ONE: DEFINE WHAT IS HAPPENING IN THE SERIES.

The first thing your child must do when he encounters a series of numbers is to find out what is going on in that series. Are the numbers increasing or decreasing? Is another number being added to them or subtracted from them? If so, how big is that number? Or are they doubling, or tripling, or halving? What is the principle that determines what the next number will be?

For example, in the series above, your child starts by asking, "What happens to five that makes it ten?" There are two answers: Either 5 more is added to it, or it is doubled.

He next goes on to the relation between 10 and 20. He asks himself, "What happens to 10 that makes it 20?" Again there are two possible answers: Either 10 more is added to it, or it is doubled.

Now he has a pattern. The number 5 was doubled to make 10, and 10 was doubled to make 20. He now believes that he knows *what is going on* in the series: each number is doubled to make the next.

He now tests this pattern on the next number. It is 40. The number 20 is doubled to make 40, so it fits. The pattern still holds.

If the pattern is correct, the next number should be 80. But it's 50 instead. So he goes on to:

STEP TWO: LOCATE THE WRONG ITEMS AND CROSS THEM OUT.

The number 50 does not follow the double pattern, so he puts a light line through it—to indicate that he believes for the moment that it should be crossed out—and goes on to the next number.

This number is 60. Again, it doesn't fit the double pattern. And again he puts a light line through it and goes on to the next number.

This number is 80. Here the pattern takes over again. He has expected 80, and found it. This indicates that both 50 and 60 were wrong numbers and should be crossed out.

But, to make certain, he still has two remaining numbers to check out the pattern. He now tests each of them.

The next number is 160. The number 80 doubled is 160. The pattern fits.

The next number is 320. The number 160 doubled is 320. Again the pattern fits.

He is now certain that 50 and 60 are the wrong numbers. He crosses them out and goes on to the next question.

This same two-part technique will be used to solve the "terror of the classrooms," which is:

TYPE OF SHORT-ANSWER QUESTION 8: NUMBER SERIES

DEFINITION: The number-series question presents your child with a series of numbers again, but this time all are correct, and he is required to write down the next one or two numbers at the end of the series.

WHAT IT LOOKS LIKE: A number-series question is usually presented in groups, starting with easy ones, and ending up with the very difficult. Here is a sample you might find on any College Admission test:

1. 5   9   13   17   21   25   29   ——   ——
2. 40   30   20   10   ——
3. 6   18   54   162   486   ——   ——
4. 7   10   14   15   18   22   23   ——
5. 3   7   5   9   7   11   9   ——   ——
6. 12   8   9   14   6   20   3   ——
7. 2   4   8   3   9   27   4   ——   ——

HOW TO MASTER IT

Again, every number-series question is a two-part question. Its first part must be solved first before your child can begin to answer it finally.

Here are the two questions he must answer before he can solve any number-series question:

1. What is happening in this series? What kind of progression is going on?

2. What, then, must the next one or two numbers in this series be?

The first question must be answered correctly before he can answer the second. Therefore your child's first job in attacking any number-series question is to *discover and mark down the series pattern.*

In fact, it is so important that he thoroughly understand

this pattern that he actually marks it down on his test paper like this:

In example 1 above, he asks himself, "What happens to 5 that makes it 9?" The answers is that 4 is added to it, and he draws a line between the 5 and the 9 and marks down +4 on top of that line, like this:

$$\overset{+4}{\overbrace{5 \quad 9}}$$

Now he asks himself, "What happens to 9 that makes it 13?" The answer is again plus 4. And he again draws a line between the two numbers and marks +4 above it like this:

$$\overset{+4}{\overbrace{5}} \ \overset{+4}{\overbrace{9 \ \ 13}}$$

A physical, concrete pattern *that he can see* is now beginning to emerge before his eyes. He continues this marking of the pattern through every number in the series, until, when he has finished the first step, the question now looks like this:

$$\overset{+4}{\overbrace{5}} \ \overset{+4}{\overbrace{9}} \ \overset{+4}{\overbrace{13}} \ \overset{+4}{\overbrace{17}} \ \overset{+4}{\overbrace{21}} \ \overset{+4}{\overbrace{25}} \ 29 \ - \ -$$

The pattern is now obvious. To answer the second part of the question, he simply adds 4 to 29 to get 33, and then adds 4 again to get 37.

This same technique of marking the pattern greatly simplifies all number-series questions. In example 2, for instance, the pattern −10 emerges, and the problem looks like this:

$$\overset{-10}{\overbrace{40}} \ \overset{-10}{\overbrace{30}} \ \overset{-10}{\overbrace{20}} \ 10 \ -$$

At this point, the answer quite obviously becomes 0.

In example 3, the pattern ×3 emerges, and the problem looks like this:

$$\underbrace{}_{×3}\ \underbrace{}_{×3}\ \underbrace{}_{×3}\ \underbrace{}_{×3}$$
6   18   54   162   486 ― ―

The answers thus become 1,458 and 4,374.

But, in example 4, the pattern becomes more complicated. In examples 1, 2, and 3, the same pattern held for every number in the series. In example 1, the pattern +4 held for every number. In example 2, the pattern −10 held for every number. And in example 3, the pattern ×3 held for every number.

But in example 4, no one pattern holds throughout the series. The pattern between the first two numbers looks like this:

$$\overset{+3}{\frown}$$
7   10

The pattern between the second two numbers emerges like this:

$$\overset{+3}{\frown}\ \overset{+4}{\frown}$$
7   10   14

And the pattern between the third two numbers looks like this:

$$\overset{+3}{\frown}\ \overset{+4}{\frown}\ \overset{+1}{\frown}$$
7   10   14   15

So far there is no relation between these two-number patterns. But in the next two numbers, this pattern emerges:

$$\overset{+3}{\frown}\ \overset{+4}{\frown}\ \overset{+1}{\frown}\ \overset{+3}{\frown}$$
7   10   14   15   18

The +3 pattern has repeated itself. Is this a coincidence, or is it the beginning of a new cycle of a +3+4+1 pattern? To find out, your child tests the next two numbers. If it is a new cycle, the next pattern should be +4, and the next number should be 22:

$$\overset{+3}{\frown}\ \overset{+4}{\frown}\ \overset{+1}{\frown}\ \overset{+3}{\frown}\ \overset{+4}{\frown}$$
$$7\quad 10\quad 14\quad 15\quad 18\quad 22$$

It is, of course. And the final number should then be 23, to give this final look to the problem:

$$\overset{+3}{\frown}\ \overset{+4}{\frown}\ \overset{+1}{\frown}\ \overset{+3}{\frown}\ \overset{+4}{\frown}\ \overset{+1}{\frown}$$
$$7\quad 10\quad 14\quad 15\quad 18\quad 22\quad 23\ \ —$$

The over-all pattern has now emerged. It is a repeat of +3+4+1. Therefore, it is obvious that the next number in the series, the final answer, is obtained by adding 3 to 23 to get 26.

What your child has encountered here is a pattern composed of three different numbers, all of which are added in rotation to the numbers that occur in the series.

This new pattern is more complicated than the patterns in the first three examples, each of which had *one* number (4, 10 and 3), and *one* operation (addition, subtraction, and multiplication).

Example 4, however, though it had only one operation (addition) had three numbers.

Now, what would happen if your child were given a number series with *two* operations and *two* numbers?

This is example 5. Writing in the pattern, he gets this:

$$\overset{+4}{\frown}\ \overset{-2}{\frown}\ \overset{+4}{\frown}\ \overset{-2}{\frown}\ \overset{+4}{\frown}\ \overset{-2}{\frown}$$
$$3\quad 7\quad 5\quad 9\quad 7\quad 11\quad 9\ \ —\ \ —$$

The answer becomes obvious at once. Adding 4 to 9, he gets 13. And subtracting 2 from 13, he gets 11.

In a number series, there can be any number of operations and any number of numbers to perform them on.

But number series can get even *more* complicated. Take example 6. Marking in our single pattern, we get this:

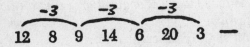

Here, there seems to be no pattern at all. And there is no *single* pattern. For a number series can also have *more* than one pattern in it. It can have two or more patterns.

But where are these patterns? Certainly not between the first and second or second and third numbers.

Then why not experiment? Why not try the first and third numbers, and then the third and fifth? And then the second and fourth numbers, and fourth and sixth?

If your child tries this, here is how his first every-other-number pattern will look:

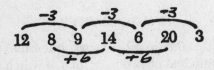

And here's how his second every-other-number pattern now looks:

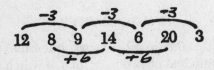

Now the patterns have emerged, and the answer is again obvious. He adds 6 to 20 and gets the correct answer, 26.

And once he gets used to the idea of two or more patterns in a single number series, even the most complicated problems of this type become a snap. In example 7, for instance, he immediately spots the pattern as being this:

$$\overbrace{\ }^{\times 2}\ \overbrace{\ }^{\times 2}\qquad \overbrace{\ }^{\times 3}\ \overbrace{\ }^{\times 3}\qquad \overbrace{\ }^{\times 4}\ \overbrace{\ }^{\times 4}$$
$$2\quad 4\quad 8\quad 3\quad 9\quad 27\quad 4\ —\ —$$

He simply multiplies 4 by 4 to get 16, and 16 by 4 to get 64, and he has the correct answer.

Again, as in all these number-series problems, the two-step technique works miracles in making the answer emerge. First, your child discovers the pattern. Then the pattern tells him the next number he needs to complete the series.

TYPE OF SHORT-ANSWER QUESTION 9: ANALOGIES

DEFINITION: An Analogy question asks your child to compare one relation between two objects to another, similar relation between two other objects. Its usual form is "this is to that as something is to something else."

WHAT IT LOOKS LIKE: *Knowledge is to judgment as possession is to* (1) *law* (2) *acquisition* (3) *use* (4) *ignorance* (5) *dispossession.*

Or, in a slightly different form:

HOURGLASS: CLOCK is most similar to:

(1) *acorn:oak* (2) *foundation:temple* (3) *temple:church* (4) *catapult:church* (5) *catapult:cannon.*

HOW TO MASTER IT

Again, like the number-series question, the analogy question is composed of two parts, one of which is stated and the other hidden.

The first step in solving an analogy question is to find, and state, the *relation* between the two objects that are given.

The second step is to choose the two objects in the answer list that have *the same relation* as the given objects.

First, your child finds the relation between the two given

objects, and writes it down just as he wrote down the hidden pattern in the number-series questions. Then he finds the other pair of objects in the answer list that have exactly the same relation.

For example, what is the relation between HOUR-GLASS and CLOCK?

An hourglass is a PRIMITIVE clock. It was the FORE-RUNNER of the clock. So this PRIMITIVE, FORERUN-NER relation is what your child is looking for. He writes it down, and begins testing each of the pairs in the answer list against it.

Acorn:oak. Not quite the same. An oak grows from an acorn, but a clock replaces an hourglass. The oak was inherent in the acorn, but a clock is an entirely different mechanism from an hourglass. Mark it no and go on.

Foundation:temple. No resemblance in the relation. A temple is built on a foundation, but a clock is not built in any way on the same foundation as an hourglass. No.

Temple:church. No. Two different houses of worship. Both exist at the present time. No resemblance.

Catapult:church. No comparison.

Catapult:cannon. This looks like it. A catapult is a PRIMITIVE cannon, just as an hourglass was a PRIMITIVE clock. A catapult was a FORERUNNER of the cannon, just as the hourglass was a FORERUNNER of the clock. This is the correct answer. He marks it down and goes on to the next question.

What is the relation between KNOWLEDGE and JUDGMENT? He puts the same technique to work:

Knowledge is a REQUIREMENT for good judgment. To be a good judge, one *must have* knowledge. This is the relation your child is looking for. He writes it down—a RE-QUIREMENT— and begins testing the pairs in the answer list against it.

Possession:law. Possession is *not* a requirement for law. No resemblance.

Possession:acquisition. Possession is *not* a requirement for acquisition. They are practically synonymous. No resemblance.

Possession:use. Possession *is* a requirement for use. You must possess something to use it. This looks like the correct answer. Your child checks it off, but still goes on to each of the other possibilities to make absolutely certain.

Possession:ignorance. No resemblance at all.

Possession:dispossession. No resemblance. They mean exactly the opposite.

Therefore it must be *possession:use.* The correct answer emerges, once the hidden relation is brought out into the open.

TYPE OF SHORT-ANSWER QUESTION 10: THE COMBINATION QUESTION

Finally, of course, many of the questions your child will encounter on his examinations will be combinations of one or two of the types described above.

These combination questions can always be solved by the step-by-step method. They are first broken down into the number of steps it takes to solve them, and then each step is done in its turn.

For example, take this question from a typical grade-school geography quiz:

Select the third letter of the word which correctly completes the following statement: Chicago is located in the state of

(1) -I (2) -A (3) -N (4) -L (5) -O

There are two parts to this question. First, to find the state in which Chicago is located, which is *Illinois*. Then, to find the third letter of the word, *Illinois,* which is -L. Thus the correct answer is 4.

Though the question may have seemed hard or confusing when your child first encountered it, it becomes simple as soon as he breaks it down step by step.

A FINAL NOTE ON A VERY SPECIAL TYPE OF TEST: HOW TO RAISE YOUR CHILD'S I.Q.

Throughout his school career your child will be judged by, not one, but two separate systems of grading him.

The first system, of course, will be his results in the exams he is given.

The second system of grading him will be his results in the I.Q. tests he will be given from time to time.

There is nothing mysterious or Godlike or absolutely final about an I.Q. test. It is just another kind of test. What it measures is not really your child's innate intelligence, but simply his ability to pass this type of test.

Therefore, as in any other test, his grades can be improved by planning and practice. And, since this is probably the most important single test he will ever take in his school career, let us right now examine each one of the types of questions he will encounter on it, and how he can improve his performance on them:

1. Synonyms. Select the word which means the same. Sample:

BABY: 1. son; 2. child; 3. sister; 4. born.

Technique:

1. Think of our synonym before you read the list. 2. Read the entire list, crossing out wrong possibilities, and matching your answer to the answer on the list.

2. Antonyms. Select the word which means the opposite.

Sample:

BACK: 1. side; 2. front; 3. top.

Technique:

1. Think of our synonym before you read the list. 2. Think of the word that means exactly the opposite. 3. Read the entire answer list to find this word and cross out the others.

3. Classification. Verbal cross outs. Cross out the word

that does not belong with the others.

Sample:

A. *daisy*; B. *rose*; C. *cat*; D. *lily*.

Technique:

1. Read the entire list to discover the over-all classification. 2. Write down the name of the classification. 3. Go over every word, crossing out the one that does not belong.

Warning:

Beware of the first word on the list. It may be the wrong one. Therefore read the entire list before deciding on the over-all classification.

4. *Logical reasoning.* Special type of multiple choice. Select the word which tells what the first word *always* has.

Sample:

BOOK: A. *pictures*; B. *pages*; C. *cover*; D. *story*.

Warning:

Key word here is *always*. Not *sometimes* or *may possibly*. But *always—without fail*. Therefore, even though a book may *sometimes* have pictures, or a cover, or a story, it only has, *without fail*, pages, or it could not be a book.

Technique:

1. Ask immediately, before reading the list, "A book *could only* be a book, *without fail*, if it had ——." 2. Write down the answer. 3. Read the entire list, matching your own answer, and crossing out the other possibilities as they do not fit.

5. *Number sequence.* Filling in the next number in a given series.

Sample:

What number should come next?

2   4   6   8   10   12   ——

Technique:

1. Find out *what happens* in the series—establish the pattern between each of the numbers in the series. 2. Use this pattern to show you the next number.

6. *Analogies.* Given two objects with a specific relation, find a similar relation in two other objects.

Sample:

Gun is to shoot as knife is to: A. fly; B. meat; C. hurt; D. cut; E. hit.

Technique:

Again, use two steps. 1. Define the relation between the two given objects, and write it down. 2. Find the same relation between one of the possible answers, eliminating each of the others as you read it.

7. *Proverbs.* A kind of analogy. Given a famous proverb, find another statement among those furnished which means the same or most nearly the same.

Sample:

DO NOT HANG ALL ON ONE NAIL.

A. *Don't count your chickens until they're hatched.*

B. *Don't put all your eggs in one basket.*

C. *Don't use a nail, use a hanger.*

Technique:

1. After reading the given proverb, before you read the answer list, try to rephrase it in more general terms (for instance, in this example, try: "Don't risk all on one chance"). 2. Read each of the possibilities, to find the one that matches your own rephrasing.

These, then, are the seven most used types of questions given on I.Q. tests. To help your child get the top possible grades he is capable of getting on these tests, go over these types of questions with him again and again. Make up new examples. Be sure he can use the right technique on each of them as easily as he can write his own name.

In summary:

Your child will encounter these ten types of short-answer questions on his tests:

True-false.	Analogies.
Multiple-choice.	Number series.
Completion.	Cross out.
Matching.	Sequence.
Enumeration.	Combinations.

Through applying the proper techniques, each of these questions can be made simple, and even help to furnish all or part of its own answer.

By giving your child practice, and more practice in solving each of them, you will turn him into a test-room champion.

CHAPTER 24

HOW TO MASTER THE ESSAY TEST

The second great category of test that your child will have to deal with in his examination room is the essay test.

The essay test requires your child to write. It confronts him with a question, or a series of questions, that demand lengthy, organized answers that may take up a full written page or more.

It tests his ability to:

1. Organize his ideas, and
2. Express them clearly and logically on paper.

Therefore, on the essay test, he is graded on two accomplishments:

1. What he says, and
2. How he says it.

Let us see how we can help him get better grades in both these areas.

THE BASIC STRATEGY IN TAKING AN ESSAY TEST

We will, of course, assume that your child has prepared for the test in the manner outlined in this book. In other words, that he has absorbed and organized the material, arranged it in notes, reviewed the notes to eliminate any misunderstandings, and, above all, quizzed himself on the information in those notes by creating and answering a series of essay-type questions of his own.

Because of this preparation, then, when he enters the exam room he is ready, not only with thoroughly organized material, but with some of the very questions that he will be asked on the test.

With this bedrock background, he follows this procedure:

1. He first reads the complete list of questions. In some essay exams, only one or two or three questions may make up the entire test. In others, there may be as many as ten questions, each demanding only a paragraph or two.

In any case, he carefully reads them all, asking himself these two primary questions:

"Do I have to answer all the questions that are asked on this test, or does the test give me a choice?"

"Either way, how many questions will I have to answer in the time I have allotted for this test?"

2. Let us say, for example, that there are five essay questions that your child must answer on his test. Once he has determined this fact, he now proceeds to *ration his time.* He does it in this way:

He determines the total amount of time he will have for the test—let us say two hours, or one hundred and twenty minutes. He first allows himself twenty minutes at the end of this two hours, to review what he has written and to correct any errors that he might have overlooked the first time.

This leaves him with one hundred minutes of writing, in which he will have to answer five questions. Therefore he allots twenty minutes to each question.

He now has his over-all time schedule set up. He now turns to the individual questions.

3. If the test does not demand that he do the questions in a specific order, he arranges them in order himself. He does the easiest question first. The second-easiest second, and so on.

4. Now, each individual question gets its own time schedule. Each of these answers has two steps :

First it is outlined.

Then it is written.

The outline is easily as important as the final written

answer. It is in this outline that he builds the idea backbone of his answer. That he organizes the thoughts that he will later put into sentences.

Therefore, for each answer, he should take about one-fifth of his time to outline the answer, and the rest to write it out on the basis of that outline.

For example, four minutes to outline his answer and sixteen minutes of guided writing will give him a far better grade than a mere twenty minutes of blind writing. And the organization of his thoughts will shine right through.

And, above all, this way he won't write himself into a corner, where he finds he's just beginning to answer the question when the exam time is almost over.

Now, let's take a look at some of the essay questions he will be required to answer, and what he must do to get each one of them precisely right.

THE KEY ESSAY-QUESTION WORDS, AND HOW TO ANSWER EACH OF THEM CORRECTLY

KEY WORD:
1. *Evaluate.*
SAMPLE QUESTION:
Evaluate the concept of "overlearning" as a sound study procedure.
WHAT TO DO TO ANSWER IT CORRECTLY:
An evaluation is an appraisal, a weighing of pros and cons. Therefore your child's answer should cite the advantages and disadvantages of the subject being discussed, and end with his opinion on its worth.

KEY WORD:
2. *Summarize.*
SAMPLE QUESTION:
Summarize the main economic causes of World War I.
WHAT TO DO TO ANSWER IT CORRECTLY:

A summary is a condensed outline of main points. Therefore your child should give *the main points only* in a concise, outline form, omitting minor detail. Here, the bare outline will often do for the answer, if he is in a hurry.

KEY WORD:
3. *Compare.*
SAMPLE QUESTION:
Compare standardized and teacher-made tests in respect to use in the classroom.
WHAT TO DO TO ANSWER IT CORRECTLY:
A comparison is an examination of character or qualities, for the purpose of discovering resemblances or differences. Therefore your child should first list the qualities of each of the two subjects to be compared, and then show how they resemble each other, or how they differ from each other. He is not required to evaluate them, or end up with an opinion on their comparative worth.

KEY WORD:
4. *Explain.*
SAMPLE QUESTION:
Explain the concept of a chain reaction.
WHAT TO DO TO ANSWER IT CORRECTLY:
To explain is to make plain. Therefore your child should show exactly how the subject works, in logical, step-by-step order. This happens, which causes this to happen, which causes this to happen.

KEY WORD:
5. *Criticize.*
SAMPLE QUESTION:
Criticize the statement, "One should study at least two hours for every hour spent in class."
WHAT TO DO TO ANSWER IT CORRECTLY:
A criticism is an examination of a subject and then a

judgment. Therefore your child should first examine the evidence for and against the statement, and then give his opinion on its merits.

KEY WORD:
6. *Name.*
SAMPLE QUESTION:
Name three factors that are basic to school success.
WHAT TO DO TO ANSWER IT CORRECTLY:
This is the easiest and shortest of all essay questions. Your child simply names the subjects asked for, without further detail.

KEY WORD:
7. *Discuss.*
SAMPLE QUESTION:
Discuss the role of the liver in digestion.
WHAT TO DO TO ANSWER IT CORRECTLY:
To discuss something is to examine it from all angles. Therefore your child should give the complete story of the subject asked for, from its beginning to its end.

KEY WORD:
8. *Outline.*
SAMPLE QUESTION:
Outline the principal steps in preparing an assignment.
WHAT TO DO TO ANSWER IT CORRECTLY:
Your child has been outlining all year long. Therefore he simply uses his primary outline as the final answer to this question.

KEY WORD:
9. *List.*
SAMPLE QUESTION:
List five suggestions that are applicable to preparing for examinations.

WHAT TO DO TO ANSWER IT CORRECTLY:

A listing is simply a naming. Therefore your child numbers the subjects asked for, and names them one after the other without further elaboration.

KEY WORD:

10. *Define.*

SAMPLE QUESTION:

Define the term "expletive."

WHAT TO DO TO ANSWER IT CORRECTLY:

A definition is the explanation of the meaning of a word. Therefore your child starts his definition with, "An (expletive) is . . . ," and explains its meaning in the remainder of the sentence. Few words will require more than one sentence.

KEY WORD:

11. *State.*

SAMPLE QUESTION:

State three reasons for Red China's being barred from the United Nations.

WHAT TO DO TO ANSWER IT CORRECTLY:

To state is the same as to name. Therefore your child uses the same procedure as that discussed above.

KEY WORD:

12. *Review.*

SAMPLE QUESTION:

Review the principal causes of the Stock Market crash of 1929.

WHAT TO DO TO ANSWER IT CORRECTLY:

Same as discuss. Use same procedure.

KEY WORD:

13. *Describe.*

SAMPLE QUESTION:

Describe the circulatory system of the human body.

WHAT TO DO TO ANSWER IT CORRECTLY:

A description is simply a narration without searching for causes. Therefore your child simply follows through the process asked for, step by step, without giving any reasons for its cause or order.

KEY WORD:
14. *Enumerate.*
SAMPLE QUESTION:
Enumerate the results of Soviet Russia's walling off of East Berlin from the West.
WHAT TO DO TO ANSWER IT CORRECTLY:
To enumerate is to list or name. Therefore your child uses the technique described above.

KEY WORD:
15. *Illustrate.*
SAMPLE QUESTION:
Give three illustrations of President Eisenhower's foreign policy during his term in office.
WHAT TO DO TO ANSWER IT CORRECTLY:
To illustrate is to give examples. Therefore your child names the number of examples required, describing them sufficiently to identify them, but neither evaluating them nor giving causes for their existence.

KEY WORD:
16. *Interpret.*
SAMPLE QUESTION:
Interpret the Supreme Court ruling on integration in the University of Mississippi Case.
WHAT TO DO TO ANSWER IT CORRECTLY:
An interpretation is an explanation, usually in reference to a specific instance or viewpoint. Therefore your child explains the consequence of the subject (in this case, the Supreme Court ruling) in the instance asked for (in this case, the University of Mississippi dispute).

KEY WORD:

17. *Justify.*

SAMPLE QUESTION:

Justify the statement, "All behavior is ultimately caused by circumstances outside the individual."

WHAT TO DO TO ANSWER IT CORRECTLY:

A justification is a marshaling of reasons for a cause or statement. Therefore your child lists each of the facts that prove the statement given, and shows how they combine to make it true.

KEY WORD:

18. *Prove.*

SAMPLE QUESTION:

What is the proof for the second law of thermodynamics?

WHAT TO DO TO ANSWER IT CORRECTLY:

Proof is double evidence—first that a statement is correct, and second that an opposite statement must be false. Therefore your child lists the facts that serve as evidence for the given statement, and then supplements them with further facts that disprove any contradictory statements.

KEY WORD:

19. *Contrast.*

SAMPLE QUESTION:

Contrast standardized and teacher-made tests in respect to use in the classroom.

WHAT TO DO TO ANSWER IT CORRECTLY:

To contrast two objects is to bring out their differences. Therefore your child should list the differences between the two objects mentioned in the question, difference by difference. He is not required to list their similarities or evaluate them.

TIPS ON RAISING YOUR CHILD'S ANSWERS ABOVE THE ORDINARY LEVEL

Once your child has identified the exact way he will respond to each key word, and outlined his answer to each question, he then proceeds to write out his answers on the test paper. To improve his grades he follows these simple rules:

5. He should not use handwriting tricks. He should write clearly and neatly, with large indentions at the beginning of each paragraph.

6. For every answer, he should adopt a position and then stick to it. This position should be declared in the first sentence of each answer, in this way:

"Teacher-made tests are far superior to standardized tests for the following reasons: . . ."

7. He should document each answer, where possible, with detailed supporting evidence. Once he has memorized his backbone facts, then many concrete details will be carried along in his memory with them. He should use these details everywhere they occur, to be as specific as he can.

For example, he should not say:

"Man needs a certain minimum daily food intake."

If he has the information to say:

"A man weighing 165 pounds needs as many as 4,500 calories per day."

This adds color and believability to his main points. But make sure he gets the main points down first, and then fills in the details.

8. Certain easy-to-do devices add great excitement and believability to his answers—make his examination paper stand out head and shoulders above the common crowd. Have him use as many of the following devices as possible:

A. Diagrams.
B. Graphs.
C. Outlines.

D.   Underlined sections.

E.   Technical terms.

F.   Illustrations and examples.

9.   Cross references save time, squeeze more information into each question, impress readers. They are a simple method of quoting part of one question to help document another.

For example, he might use a cross reference in this way: *"Teacher-made tests are also superior to the standardized version for the reasons stated in answers 2 (b) and 3 (c) given above."*

10.   There is no reason for him to argue with the position taken by the teacher in the exam statements. He should take the teacher's position as his own and develop it as given.

11.   And he should never, never use slang. He should use good English and good logic throughout.

WHAT HE DOES IN THE LAST TWENTY MINUTES

12.   He saves the last twenty minutes as a safety factor. When he reaches them, he stops writing, no matter how far along he is in the test.

13.   If he has finished all the answers, he now carefully reads them, correcting spelling and punctuation, checking them against his outline to make sure he has included every main point.

If he wishes to add a final idea, he does so at the bottom of the question, beginning it with a statement such as:

"One further point that increases the superiority of teacher-made tests even further . . ."

14.   If, however, he has not finished that "one last question," he uses half this twenty minutes to fill it in in this way:

He makes a formal outline of the answer. He touches on all aspects of the answer in this formal outline, using clear, concise sentences for each main point. If his outline is valid and clear enough, and if his other answers show a mature writing style, he may receive full credit for this outline answer as well.

15. Above all, he should use every second of time allowed by the test to make sure his answers are the absolute best he can make them.

In all these answers, he should give exactly what is called for. Neither more nor less than is expected. Clear, concise, to the point. And then go on to the next question.

In summary:

Essay tests are graded on two separate accomplishments:

Your child's ability to:

1. Organize his ideas, and
2. Express them clearly and logically.

Therefore, to get top grades on an essay test, a plan of attack is essential.

One-fifth of his time should be devoted to outline his answers, three-fifths of his time to writing out those outline answers, and the remaining one-fifth of his time to checking that writing to remove any omissions or errors.

Each answer should give exactly what is called for in the question. Therefore he should know what each essay-test key word demands from him, and be immediately ready to satisfy it.

CHAPTER 25

THE SIMPLE STRATEGY OF MAKING THE TEST
ITSELF HELP YOUR CHILD PASS

Now that your child is familiar with the types of questions that he will encounter in his tests, and has been drilled in the proper way to answer each of them, let us now bring all these test-taking skills together, and see how he uses them to pull out a top grade in an actual examination.

We have already done this for an essay-type test. Now we will set up the same strategy—the same professional time schedule—for the hundreds of short-answer tests he will take during his lifetime.

Here he goes. On his way to another test-taking triumph.

THE FIRST FIVE MINUTES

His first goal, when he enters the room, is always to overcome whatever emotional excitement he may have brought with him. He wants to take this test calmly and coolly, in complete charge of all the information he has prepared.

For this reason, the first five minutes are crucial. It is during these five minutes that he either settles himself down to productive work, and makes the test work for him, or gives way to panic and mind-blocking. In order to avoid this, he follows this simple procedure:

1. He lays his pencil down on the desk, and does not pick it up for five minutes.

2. He uses this five minutes to *pre-read* the exam. To become familiar with the entire exam before he does any part of it. To read all directions *twice*. To look especially for the following points:

A. What are the exact instructions? Are the answers to be given in any special way? Is there a choice of questions, or does every question have to be answered?

B. Are there any questions that he anticipated? If so, they will give a big boost to his confidence.

C. How long is the exam? Will there be a time problem? If so, he will start on the easiest or most familiar questions, skipping those he doesn't know and coming back to them later if he has the time.

D. What parts of the exam give the most credit? These he will do first, if he knows them.

E. Are there any questions that are closely related? If so, he will make sure he doesn't give the same answer on both.

F. Do any questions give the answer, or suggest the answer, to another question? This happens far too often to be overlooked, and can add as much as 10 per cent to 15 per cent to his grade.

3. All these pre-reading questions must be answered *before* your child picks up his pen actually to begin writing the exam.

At this point he will be calm, confident, and deliberate, without a trace of the emotional overexcitement that could spell disaster.

WRITING THE EXAM: HOW TO AVOID THE 20 PER CENT OF CARELESS ERRORS THAT MOST STUDENTS MAKE

In the actual writing of the exam, of course, the second great danger occurs. This is plain ordinary carelessness, the malady that causes more test failures than anything else but sheer neglect of study.

Here are some of the most frequent mistakes caused by nothing else but sheer carelessness:

The student fails to read the question *correctly*. He misses key words, or misses their meaning.

The student reads only *part* of a question, and then starts to answer without reading the rest of the question. But that last part of the question may change its meaning entirely.

The student makes a list when he's asked to explain. Or gives incidents and events, rather than the causes for them. Or compares when he's asked to contrast. Or writes long, detailed lists of reasons, when he's asked to give the main reason only.

Such patterns of carelessness are constant. When your child develops one of them, he will repeat it over and over again, unless you help him stamp it out.

Therefore, as we have said before, study your child's *particular pattern of carelessness* BEFORE he gets in the test room. And then correct it, day by day, till it is completely eradicated, and he will never slip back into it, even under the most extreme pressure.

WRITING THE EXAM: MAKING SURE THAT EACH ANSWER IS CORRECT

4. Now your child picks up his pencil and begins to answer the test. His first step is to go back to the questions he is sure of, and answer them first.

5. He uses these correct answers, plus the information given him in the other test questions, plus the techniques of making questions solve themselves that we have described in Chapter 22, to work through the remaining questions that he is not completely sure of.

6. He solves them one question at a time. He reads each twice to make sure he understands it. He concentrates on it exclusively, without glancing at the remaining questions till he has finished it. Then he goes on to the next one.

7. He strives for neatness, good order, correct spelling, grammar, and punctuation where required.

8. He tries to allot himself five or ten minutes after he

has finished the test to review it. He uses this time to check back over the test to make sure there are no careless mistakes or omissions. He does not, however, "second-guess" his answers; he relies on his first intuitive answer unless he has uncovered new information further along in the test that makes him sure that he has a better answer.

9. If there are answers still unfinished, or questions he does not know, he follows this rule:

If the test does not penalize for guessing or wrong answers, and if an unanswered question will be graded wrong anyway, then he makes the best possible guess.

If, however, the test penalizes for guessing in any way, he simply leaves the questions blank.

10. Again, he uses every second of the time given to him by the test. He checks and rechecks to make sure he has made no correctible mistakes, no omissions, that he has squeezed out the absolute top grade he is capable of.

And then he hands the paper in and forgets it. Because he knows that he has done his job—done it well—and he can confidently await his reward.

A reward that you should make absolutely sure you echo when the final grades are in!

In summary:

In taking any test, your child must first concentrate on eliminating:

1. Overexcitement and emotional block.
2. Careless mistakes.

Once he has done this, he then concentrates on making one part of the test help him solve the other, as we have shown you in these chapters.

These three basic techniques add up to top grades on any test that can be thrown at your child. Exercised properly, they give him an enormous advantage over any other student in that test room.

EPILOGUE

HOW TO MAKE YOUR CHILD INTO A CLASSROOM CHAMPION

There it is. You now have the techniques you need to double your child's grades in school.

They are simple, fast, and enormously effective. Used properly, they can get him into the Rapid-Advancement Class that might otherwise reject him, can get him the A's and B's that he might otherwise have just barely missed, can get him into the college of his choice and the job of his dreams that might otherwise have passed him by.

But they can't do a darned one of these things without your active support!

Reading these techniques—even learning them—is just not enough. Teaching them to your child is not enough. Even demanding that he memorize them is not enough.

They are no good to you—or him—until they become SECOND NATURE to him. Until they are built into the nervous system of your child as reaction patterns or habits. Until he does them automatically—perfectly—without thinking. As easily and quickly and naturally as he now writes his name.

And this means PRACTICE!

PRACTICE!

PRACTICE!

Champions in any field, whether it be art, or sports, or business, or study, are made by two great tools:

1. Knowledge or technique.
2. Practice to perfect that technique.

The first element, knowledge, can be bought. It can be bought in the form of a book, or a lecture, or even in the form of hard experience.

But the second element, practice, can only be earned. It is a function of character. It is a result of that inner drive, persistence, endurance, patience, will to win, inability to quit, that makes the champion.

In life, it is not intelligence that makes the great difference. We have all seen too many brilliant minds left panting behind—shattered and defeated—doomed to lives of nameless mediocrity.

In life, ultimately, *it is drive that counts!* The tortoise still wins; the hare still is left sleeping in obscurity!

"*A winner never quits; a quitter never wins.*"

"*Practice makes perfect.*"

This is old wisdom. True wisdom. Wisdom that works today in the science laboratory as much as it did in the groves of Socratic Greece.

Teach it to your child. Build into your child, not only the techniques that produce success, but the drive that will settle for nothing less than success, and you will give him— or her—the greatest gift next to love that it will ever be in your power to hand on.

Good luck. And good teaching.

INDEX